I0813696
The Regenerative Gardener's Handbook

The Regenerative Gardener's Handbook
Essential Techniques for Growing a Garden That Leaves the Land Healthier Than You Found It
BY BRIANA SELSTAD BOSCH
Storey Publishing

The mission of Storey Publishing is to serve our customers by publishing practical information that encourages personal independence in harmony with the environment.

EDITED BY Kristen Hewitt and Carleen Madigan
ART DIRECTION AND BOOK DESIGN BY Michaela Jebb
BACK COVER DESIGN BY Bredna Lago
TEXT PRODUCTION BY Jennifer Jepson Smith

COVER PHOTOGRAPHY BY © Bonnie Sen Photography, except BC (b. & 2nd fr. b.) by © Briana Selstad Bosch
INTERIOR PHOTOGRAPHY BY © **Bonnie Sen Photography**, i–iii, v, vi t.l. & t.r., viii, 1, 3–4, 7, 12, 14 b. & t.r., 15 r., 17 r., 18 l., 23, 25–27, 29 r. (all), 31 t., 32, 33 l., 42, 48, 52–53, 57–58, 61, 66, 78 l., 81–90, 92, 94, 96, 97 l., 98 l., 100 all but t.r., 101, 102 r., 103, 104 r., 105 b., 107 r., 108 b.r., 109, 112–114, 120, 131 r., 134 b. & t.r., 135 t., 140, 145, 149 t., 150–151, 155, 162–165, 167–168, 169 t.l. & t.r., 172 l., 173, 175 t., 177 t.l., 179, 181, 184–193, 195–199, 201–202, 220; © **Briana Selstad Bosch**, vi b.l. & b.r., 2, 6, 8–10, 14 t.l., 15 l., 16, 17 l., 18 r., 19–22, 24, 28, 29 b.l., 30, 31 b., 33 r., 34, 36, 37 l., 38, 40 b., 41, 43, 45–46, 51, 54–55, 63, 65, 68–69, 71–73, 75–77, 78 r., 79, 95, 97 r., 98 r., 99, 100 t.r., 102 l., 104 c. & l., 105 t., 106, 107 l., 108 b.l., 111, 115–119, 121–123, 126–130, 131 l., 132–133, 134 t.l., 135 b., 137, 141–144, 146–148, 149 b., 152, 154, 156 l., 157, 166, 169 b., 170, 172 r., 174, 175 b., 176, 177 t.r. & b., 178, 180, 204
Additional photography by Dorothea Lange/Farm Security Administration/Office of War Information Photograph Collection/Library of Congress, 161; © Pictorial Press Ltd/Alamy Stock Photo, 160; © robertharding/Alamy Stock Photo, 37 r.; Robin Cain, 108 t.; © Vinokurov Alexandr /Shutterstock.com, 156 r.; © Zoonar GmbH /Alamy Stock Photo, 40 t.

Storey Publishing
210 MASS MoCA Way
North Adams, MA 01247
storey.com

Storey Publishing is an imprint of Workman Publishing, a division of Hachette Book Group, Inc., 1290 Avenue of the Americas, New York, NY 10104. The Storey Publishing name and logo are registered trademarks of Hachette Book Group, Inc.

ISBNs: 978-1-63586-854-8 (paperback); 978-1-63586-855-5 (ebook)

Printed in China by Toppan Leefung Printing Ltd. on paper from responsible sources
10 9 8 7 6 5 4 3 2 1

TLF

Library of Congress Cataloging-in-Publication Data on file

For my steadfast husband, Dave, and my sweet girls, Caisa and Cora—thank you for believing in me and my wild dream to change the gardening world.

To my parents, who handed me my first patch of earth and every tool I needed to grow—both in soil and in spirit.

And to my angels above, Emily and Korinna—your loss rooted me in the healing arms of nature and planted the seed of this work.

CONTENTS

INTRODUCTION

Tending a garden is one of the most rewarding, soul-nourishing, and therapeutic endeavors. The smell of the moist, dark, loamy soil, warmed by the sun and dampened by spring rains, is invigorating. There is a simple joy in plucking a perfectly ripened, sun-kissed, juicy cherry tomato off a vine and feeling its warmth in your hand, then kneeling down to pull an eager weed (or 20). The gentle symphony of birdsong accompanies morning strolls through the garden along with the mesmerizing dance of bees flitting from flower to flower.

As recently as three generations ago, gardening was not only a way of life, it was a means of survival. Our great-grandparents canned and preserved, stored and saved seed not as a hobby but as a necessity to feed their families. Homegrown produce was fresh, healthy, and inexpensive; and gardening was then what today we would call environmentally conscious. People ate what was in season because that's what was available: Berries, tomatoes, peppers, beans, and fresh produce from the garden were consumed and preserved in summer. Apples, potatoes, squash, and root vegetables were stored in cold cellars in fall and eaten over winter, along with preserved foods.

Today, grocery stores brim with offseason produce even in the darkest days of winter. Chilean grapes, tropical fruits from Vietnam, berries from Mexico: Our perishable produce is now flown fresh on jumbo jets and carried on refrigerated trucks for thousands of miles, to the detriment of not only its nutritional quality but also the planet.

The Environmental Costs of Industrial Agriculture

In 1975, less than 5% of the fresh vegetables consumed in the United States were imported. By 2021, that number increased to 50% to 60% for fresh fruit and 20% to 38% for fresh vegetables, according to the USDA Economic Research Service. Similarly, nearly 80% of the fresh flowers sold in the States are imported from South American countries such as Ecuador and Colombia (an after-effect of trade agreements and tariff cuts implemented by the US government at the expense of American flower growers). This reliance on foreign imports comes at a steep environmental cost.

A large carbon footprint. Due to the high perishability of fresh produce and flowers, they must be shipped quickly—which means a larger carbon footprint. By United Nations estimates, growing and processing food accounts for one third of all greenhouse gas emissions, and moving produce generates twice the amount of CO_2 as growing it.

Destruction of ecosystems and soil. It's not just CO_2 emissions in transport we should be concerned with: In many parts of the world where our produce is imported from, large swaths of grassland and forest have been cleared for grazing and farming, leading to soil erosion and contamination. Our domestic agriculture isn't doing much better: Tillage and overwork of the soil leads to an average topsoil loss of approximately 5.8 tons per acre per year, while it takes an estimated 1,000 years to build 1 inch of topsoil.

Pesticide residues. Of more concern: A 2015 Food and Drug Administration report indicated that almost 10% of imported fruit violated regulations for pesticide residue, compared to 2.2% of that domestically grown. And pesticide use is increasing globally each year—including in our home gardens. This comes at a time when insects are struggling more than ever in recorded history. A 2019 study published in *Biological Conservation* found that 40% of all insect species globally are in decline, and one third are endangered. This decline sends shock waves through global ecosystems and will inevitably impact human health as well.

Increasingly, pesticides, fertilizers, and herbicides are also sold to home growers, as companies that make agricultural products recognize the potential revenue in the home gardening market. Expensive bottled and bagged "solutions" have become the usual recommendation for every problem in the garden. At every turn, we are offered conflicting advice and information, resulting in expensive gardens at best and damaged soil at worst.

These fresh, pesticide-free cherry tomatoes were harvested straight from the garden.

Are Home Gardens Any Better for the Environment?

Although it may seem that farms are to blame for environmental degradation, we home gardeners have a part to play. Urban farms and home gardens can provide many social and environmental benefits, but their carbon footprint is often higher than that of large-scale conventional farms. A recent study published in *Nature Cities* found that home gardens and agriculture can produce 57 percent to 75 percent more carbon emissions per serving of food than industrial farms due to the use of new materials for infrastructure, such as raised beds and greenhouses.

The carbon footprint of gardening products. The construction of garden beds using newly manufactured materials, such as steel, plastics, and commercially produced bagged soil mixes, contributes significantly to a higher carbon footprint. The production, transportation, and disposal of these materials often involve energy-intensive processes that release greenhouse gases.

In contrast, growing in-ground, or using upcycled or renewable materials like repurposed wood, locally sourced compost, or natural stone, reduces reliance on new resources and minimizes emissions. Shifting to sustainable garden practices mitigates the environmental impact of gardening, lowering its carbon footprint.

Turning back to traditional methods. We've forgotten traditional ways of gardening—the methods practiced before gardening became a profit-driven endeavor and plastic became commonplace. We've lost sight of seasonality and sustainable growing practices, at a steep cost to our planet and soils.

This all may seem depressing, but we make a real impact with our choices. It is clear that the planet would benefit from a change in trajectory, and that change starts in our own backyards and balconies: with regenerative gardening.

A Better Future Through Regenerative Gardening

Regenerative gardening is a way to garden that is more affordable than conventional methods, requires few (if any) purchased "solutions," embraces the ecosystem, and considers the repercussions of our actions on the environment around us, no matter how small our garden. It provides a way to garden in harmony with nature, and it not only supports but builds healthy ecosystems. After all, gardens have existed for thousands of years, but the synthetic amendments and ecosystem-decimating pesticides now commonly found in garden sheds are relatively new.

Before we launch into the full definition of regenerative gardening, I'd like to recognize that our current understanding of regenerative gardening originates from ancient Indigenous techniques, and we are indebted to those people who preceded us for their knowledge. Regenerative gardening combines those practices with modern knowledge of soil microbiology. This style of gardening emphasizes quiet patience, understanding for all living beings, and scientific understandings of how soil functions to create thriving gardens. It focuses on the regeneration and renewal of the ecosystem and the creation of sustainable practices. Simply put, it is the uncomplicated way of gardening that nature intended, a far cry from expensive bottled-and-bagged gardening methods. The practice considers nature to be a key partner rather than a disposable resource.

Regenerative gardening supports food security and cleaner air, water, and soil—giving us hope for a better climate future and a healthier planet.

My Grandpa Pat works in a cornfield on our family farm in Blooming Prairie, Minnesota, in 1972.

How I Came to Regenerative Gardening

The fifth generation of a farming family, my sister and I were the first who didn't grow up on the farm. Our family farm in Minnesota now grows just corn and soybeans but used to cultivate a much more diverse range of crops and livestock—wheat, oats, peas, hemp, dairy cows, pigs, chickens. This is the tale of many farms, overloaded with debt and struggling to turn profits, leaning on government subsidies of conventional crops to help buoy them through difficult times and high operating costs. As a young man, my dad saw the financial struggle his father went through. He decided to leave the farm and join the Army so he could attend college and pursue a different path. We grew up in the suburbs of Denver, far removed from the farm life.

From family farm to small-scale market farm. While I've always felt the drive and desire to farm, I long believed that not growing up on a working farm put me at a disadvantage. In 2018, I started my own small-scale market farm in Colorado to gain hands-on experience managing land holistically and sustainably. I applied my own theories plus research centered around regenerative agriculture with a twist: using the fewest inputs and as little money as possible. My lack of experience with large-scale conventional farming actually gave me a serious advantage. I didn't know much about the synthetic fertilizers, herbicides, and pesticides that are often used on farms, and I had never relied on turning the soil through tillage each year at planting time. Since I hadn't been raised using conventional farming practices, I came in with an open mind, ready to experiment.

Take care of the soil, and it will take care of you. I remember a visit to the family farm when I was around 10 years old. My dad took me out into the verdant fields, scooped up a handful of rich, loamy soil, and said, "See that? There's no other soil like this in the world. Whatever you do, take care of this soil, and it will always take care of you."

Now, nearly 30 years later, with the land rented to a farm tenant, I look at the same soil, but no longer with reverence for the effortlessness with which life had once seemed to spring from it—when I see it, my heart aches with the worry of carrying a generational farm into the next century. The soil is noticeably lighter in color. Sandier. Tests indicate it is becoming more acidic, and the farmland is noticeably sunken compared to the unplowed hedgerows surrounding it, due to erosion. The same two crops have been grown repeatedly in the soil for the last 50 years. When I drive across the Midwest on trips to the farm, the route is punctuated with winds blowing that rich topsoil across the roads and into culverts and ditches.

Every family reunion involves discussions around farming: "How're the crops looking this year?" And in a way, there is comfort in the redundancy of these conversations. But I have always wondered if the soil itself—if it were as important as my dad led me to believe—should be more central to the conversation.

It wasn't until I was much older and started my own farm that I recognized the importance of the soil beyond what I ever could have foreseen. Healthy soil can mean the success or failure of every plant. Problems with disease or insects decimating your garden plants? It's likely related to the soil. Your soil can be the secret to your success—or it can be the cause of an expensive and demoralizing failure.

Cutting the cost of gardening. For many, gardening has become a bit of a financial joke—"I grew this tomato and it only cost me $200!" is often chortled about in gardening circles. In a way, the act of gardening has become a wealthy person's hobby. It should come as no surprise that somehow corporations have capitalized on people's desire to grow their own nutritious produce. In American society, if we can monetize it, we do. But through much of the twentieth century, families were growing their own productive home gardens without the use of most of the store-bought products we have today. During the 1940s, for example, Victory Gardens were grown across the US.

On our farm, we have managed to slash our expenses and support a dynamic ecosystem by completely eliminating the use of pesticides, fungicides, and costly fertilizers. These have not been applied since the first year of our farm (before I knew better). And it turns out that producing homegrown, juicy, incredibly flavorful tomatoes by our methods is significantly cheaper than people have been led to believe.

Changing Our Beliefs Around Gardening

Many garden amendments were initially developed for agricultural use, and their spread to home gardens has had devastating effects. Home garden and lawn soils have been found to contain incredibly high levels of phosphorus and nitrogen due to over-fertilization, to the detriment of soil life as well as aquatic life, thanks to eutrophication (depletion of oxygen in the water) and algae growth from lawn fertilizer runoff.

Many people have become convinced that our own native soils are unsuitable for gardening, unfixable, and that the only way to be successful is to install costly manufactured raised beds and fill them with purchased bagged soil. This is a fallacy, and an ecologically damaging one. The complex network of soil life is responsible for mineralizing existing nutrients in the soil and converting organic matter into usable nutrients for plants to use—if we only allow it to.

Even the poorest of soils can be brought back to health. Productivity and soil health can be restored relatively quickly, on any scale—and it's much easier (and more affordable) than you might think.

As a market farmer practicing regenerative agriculture, I've spent years implementing these practices. Through my study of soil health, both through practice and through nearly religious nighttime sessions with a microscope, I've assembled this book: a true guide to regenerative, ecologically influenced gardening. The most incredible part of this method is how amazingly fulfilling it is to garden following these principles. Better yields and more successful plants are, of course, very satisfying—but even more so is the knowledge that regenerative gardening is better for the planet, more cost effective, and more emotionally fulfilling. The garden becomes a study rather than a struggle, and even failures are viewed with an investigative perspective—an excuse to delve further into the fascinating intricacies of soil health, butterfly effects, and paradigm shifts.

Before: Our new farm in Colorado had many invasive weeds, including thistles and Siberian elms, but the clay soil had potential to support great biodiversity.

This aerial view of the farm shows carefully planned native plantings around the perimeter of the main production area with pockets of habitat throughout the landscape. These plantings provide food, shelter, and breeding spaces for pollinators and beneficial insects, helping to balance pest pressure naturally.

Organic Versus Regenerative

Regenerative and organic growing practices are not the same thing. Organic growing is done using only USDA-approved organic products—but it is important to know that included in these approved products are broad-spectrum pesticides (pyrethrin, insecticidal soap, garlic oil, and other "natural" broad-spectrum pesticides that are still considered organic despite their wide-reaching impact on the ecosystem and bees in particular). Additionally, organic sources of fertilizer can still be overapplied, to the detriment of the soil life and pollinators. In many ways, organic gardening can still fall into the trap of treating symptoms rather than addressing root causes. It's a step in the right direction, but it's not the final destination.

Prioritizing the Health of the Ecosystem

Regenerative gardening, on the other hand, focuses on growing and regenerating soil and the garden as a piece of a living system—the health of which is always central, with the successful garden as a by-product. Regenerative gardening practices mean no pesticide sprays or granules and zero synthetic fertilizers: These chemical products interfere with the natural processes of the soil and delicate ecosystems. Most importantly, the health of the soil and ecosystem is always the main focus—this is the key we will return to throughout this guide. This method invites a shift in thinking from control to collaboration, from intervention to observation.

For this method to be successful, it becomes necessary to reprogram your modern gardening mind. Leave behind your preconceptions of what gardening is before you read on. This book will not answer questions like, "What product can I use to fix this problem?"

For regenerative gardening to be successful, you must reprogram your modern gardening mind.

Trellised tomatoes grow alongside a backdrop of sunflowers; the lavender and native Rocky Mountain ninebark in the foreground attract pollinators and beneficial insects.

Instead you'll learn to think analytically about your garden, its surrounding ecosystem, and your practices. Gardening this way will give you a more environmentally resilient, pest-resistant, and self-sustaining garden.

Blossom and Branch Farm, where we live and garden, was born from the desire to grow alongside nature, to see if our garden could thrive without amendments, fertilizers, fungicides, and pesticides—for the health of our garden and our planet, but also out of concern for cost. Starting up a large garden of more than an acre can get expensive quickly, and my husband and I had been saddled with hundreds of thousands of dollars in student loan debt from graduate school. While I used to resent the need for thriftiness, I'm now so grateful that I was forced to learn to grow this way: Not only is it more affordable, but it is also better for the garden ecosystem and the environment as a whole. Today we grow over an acre of cut flowers and produce for our community, and 40 percent of our farm is dedicated wildlife habitat that we have planted with native chokecherries, plums, apples, willows, and meadow plants.

Implementing this gardening method has been a complete flip from the way we were always told to garden. In the regenerative garden, we look to nature's processes and systems to let it dictate the best way to approach issues we may encounter along the way. The eight chapters of this book outline the key principles of the regenerative gardening mindset through which you can reframe your perspective on how to garden alongside nature.

I hope that after reading this book, you feel a renewed excitement for gardening through regenerative practices and have a revived sense of possibility for your garden—as well as a healthy skepticism of the garden industry. Welcome to regenerative gardening.

Organic Versus Regenerative

While both organic and regenerative gardens prioritize ecological principles and seek to minimize potential damage to pollinators and soil health, regenerative gardening goes a step further by aiming to actively restore and enhance natural systems and ecosystems.

Organic Garden	Regenerative Garden
Avoids synthetic pesticides, herbicides, and fertilizers. Can include broad-spectrum "organic" certified pesticides.	Goes beyond organic practices to actively regenerate soil health and ecosystem function.
Relies on natural methods like composting, crop rotation, and beneficial insects for pest control.	Adds a focus on restoring degraded landscapes and improving ecosystem resilience.
Emphasizes soil health through practices such as adding organic matter, avoiding chemical additives, and promoting microbial biodiversity.	Seeks to additionally sequester atmospheric carbon and mitigate climate change through regenerative practices such as cover cropping, no-till farming, agroforestry, and livestock integration.
Can utilize plastic mulches to the detriment of soil health.	Attempts to eliminate plastic mulches that contaminate soil or lead to reduced soil function and instead focuses on natural mulches to suppress weeds, retain moisture, and build soil organic matter.
Organic production places no limits or descriptions on whether tillage is utilized or how frequently.	Considers the environmental impact of each input added to the garden through a holistic approach.

1

Recognize the Garden as Its Own Ecosystem

FOR MUCH OF THE LAST CENTURY, we've been taught to think of production in the garden as a process involving inputs and outputs: nitrogen in, corn out. Regenerative gardening recognizes that the garden is a complex ecosystem of interdependent organisms—of which humans are just one. Understanding the ecosystem of the garden and using practices that support it will create a more self-sustaining garden, with healthier plants and soil and fewer pests.

Before: My first efforts at the farm were heavily influenced by what I saw others doing, including using landscape fabrics.

After: After four years of regenerative practices, native chokecherries and plums thrive (at right), along with golden currants (in the field at the back) and cover crops (front). We no longer use landscape fabric.

The First Season

The first growing season at the farm, we had a rough spring. I lost every single seedling I had lovingly started under lights in my basement in a freak late snowstorm, so I was thrilled when I saw that our dahlias had survived and were peeking out of the soil. I was heavily relying on them for sales, and when they started to bloom, I exulted—until I went to harvest them and found they were absolutely covered in earwigs. There were earwigs in the petals, in the creases of the leaves, and eating away the tips of the blooms before they even opened.

I was so frustrated, but I followed the advice of a fellow flower farmer and covered each bud with an organza bag before it bloomed, cinched the bag tight, and kept it on until harvest. This protected the flowers long enough that I had something to harvest, but it was so labor intensive to cover and uncover all those blooms that it was hardly profitable.

My first season on the farm, I painstakingly covered every dahlia bud with an organza bag to protect them from earwigs.

To the left of the pumpkin arbor (at center) is a hedgerow of American plums that provide a food source and habitat for birds and help keep insects like the squash vine borer at bay.

Considering the options. When I finally had time to breathe and reflect, I considered my options for dealing with the earwigs. A quick internet search recommended diatomaceous earth—but this would also kill the beneficial spiders and other ground-dwelling insects in the garden. I didn't want to do that, so I thought about why we had so many earwigs and narrowed it down to two problems. One was that the dahlias were planted too close to a wooded area, where the earwigs loved to hang out and eat decaying matter and hide in the moist crevices provided by the branches and wood chips. The other was that the rest of the property was covered in nonnative grass, which supported very few natural predators of the earwigs. I couldn't easily change the field's proximity to the woods, so instead I decided to tackle the latter problem.

Inviting native plants and birds. The following year, we removed a huge swath of grass and planted a perimeter of blue grama, yarrow, aster, and rudbeckia: natural attractants of tachinid flies, a primary predator of earwigs. We also began removing invasive plants in the wooded areas, which allowed the native chokecherries and American plums to thrive and spread; this naturally invited birds that now flood the field each spring, feasting on earwigs. Each year, once our plants are a bit larger than seedling stage, we allow our chickens free range of the field, and they dart around with gusto, digging through the mulch for their favorite earwig snack. Four years later, we no longer have to bag each individual dahlia, which has finally allowed us to grow them profitably. Instead of relying on a short-term solution via pesticides, we've invested in long-term ecosystem support, which has created inherent resiliency in the garden.

Seeing the Ecosystem at Work in Your Garden

Many of us learn about ecosystems as schoolchildren, through the study of food chains or food webs. We are taught that in order for the ecosystem to function as a whole, each piece of that system is vital—no matter how small. Without the presence of the tiniest organisms like bacteria and insects, plants and larger organisms cannot survive.

We see an example of an ecosystem breakdown in our earwig problem: A lack of biodiversity in our garden plants had subsequently led to lack of natural predators of earwigs, hence their proliferation and ability to inflict damage on our plants. If we want to support a full ecosystem, each level of that ecosystem needs to have a food source—and this includes the earwigs.

Yet, somehow, we seem to have forgotten this truth when it comes to our gardens. In the garden, we've coined terms such as *beneficial insects* and *pests*—simplifying them to "good" versus "bad" rather than considering their ecosystem function. Our second-grade selves would know better: that the "bad" bugs are simply food for other higher-chain members of the system, and that without them, the system would collapse. Yet our adult selves, obsessed with success and having perfect tomatoes, have no patience for these intricacies, and we simply seek out the quickest solution to what we see as a problem bug.

A Change in Mindset

Remember the reprogramming we said we'd be doing? What if instead of wringing our hands at the appearance of aphids in the garden we rejoiced in the abundant food source they provide for many other insects, such as our beloved ladybugs? Instead of pulling out our hair over caterpillars eating our leaves, what if we were grateful for the birds being able to feed their young with them, and for the pollinating moths and butterflies those voracious nibblers will become?

Regenerative gardening doesn't divide bugs and garden critters into the categories of "good" and "bad." They simply exist. We turn to thinking of nature as a partner, not as a resource to be consumed or a problem to be controlled. This doesn't mean that we don't need to have a thorough understanding of the garden ecosystem—on the contrary, the better we understand it, the more we can assist it.

A ladybug moves in to devour a meal of aphids on a milkweed plant.

In place of nonnative lawn grass, the landscaping here consists of native plants such as asters, baptisia, blue grama, little bluestem, and rudbeckia to attract a range of beneficial insects.

The straw mulch on this bed of asparagus plants protects soil life.

Essentials for Balancing the Garden Ecosystem

What happens when the ecosystem is lacking or is out of balance? The answer is simple: The natural balance between detrimental insects or pests and the ones who eat them (the beneficials) becomes lopsided, which leads to the majority of garden troubles, such as persistent pests, fungus, disease, and low yields.

Rather than artificially attempt to control the garden ecosystem, we would see much better results if we allowed nature to work harmoniously. Although this means that we will experience occasional crop losses and pests, the overall health and balance of the garden will improve with less effort from the gardener. But how, exactly, do we go about achieving this ecosystem balance? How can we support the function of the garden while we let nature work its beautiful balancing act? The garden ecosystem requires a symphony of parts working together. These essential components need to be supported simultaneously for the most success.

Increase Biodiversity in the Garden

Biodiversity is key to the success of the regenerative garden. Biodiversity is the presence of a wide variety of life, including plants, with an emphasis on ecosystem-supporting native life. Biodiversity includes all levels of life, from the tiniest microorganisms on up through insects and larger animals. Consider these two landscapes, which show different degrees of biodiversity.

A little wild, but full of life. One is a home garden with a large plot of native wildflowers, plants, unmown native grasses, and shrubbery surrounding a more planned and maintained garden of tomatoes, peppers, lettuces, and other plant varieties. Leaves are allowed to fall and gather around plants at season's end without being raked and thrown in the landfill. While looking slightly wild and reminiscent of a country cottage garden, this landscape provides habitats for multiple species of insects and animals.

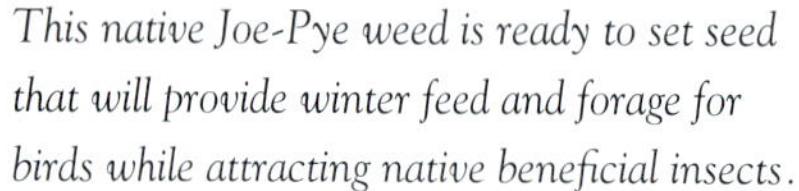

This native Joe-Pye weed is ready to set seed that will provide winter feed and forage for birds while attracting native beneficial insects.

Tomato hornworms disguise themselves among tomato plants. They can be damaging, but they also provide a host to beneficial wasps.

Neat and tidy, but less diverse. The other landscape is one we would see in a typical suburban area: a neatly mowed and edged sod lawn, with a few landscaped areas of mostly nonnative and well-pruned plants like hydrangea, roses, peonies, daylilies, and ornamental nonnative clumping grasses (which are cut down to the ground each winter). Perhaps a raised bed of edible plants such as tomatoes exists somewhere in this arrangement, almost as an island. The landscape looks neat and perpetually trimmed back. A landscape like the second one will have far less biodiversity, supporting very few insects and wildlife.

While the second landscape may fit the more socially acceptable picture of a maintained yard (and will certainly be more pleasing to most HOAs), it is also one that will see substantially more damage if hungry insects arrive. It is unrealistic to expect biodiversity in a space dominated by a nonnative monoculture like a grass lawn, particularly if it makes up the majority of the landscaping. Many lawns are kept green via lots of additional water, and frequently fertilizers and herbicides leach into waterways and lead to problems downstream and globally, all in the name of a plant that doesn't do much to support native wildlife and insects.

Utilize Biodiversity as Pest Control

Biodiversity plays a crucial role in creating a balanced garden ecosystem. In a biodiverse garden, plants attract beneficial insects and pollinators while keeping pests under control naturally. This natural pest control is essential because what we may perceive as pests are often food sources for other creatures within the soil food web. Fostering biodiversity in the garden not only enhances the overall health of plants but also supports a thriving ecosystem where every organism has its place.

HORNWORMS AS FOOD FOR PARASITIC WASPS

Look at what happens when we plant a lot of one variety of plant together. Take tomatoes, for example. If we plant all of our tomatoes in one area and our garden is discovered by the tomato hornworm (commonly considered a pest in the garden, though it actually transforms into a useful pollinating moth), those plants all become vulnerable to damage from the voracious hornworm.

Alternatively, if we intersperse our tomatoes with squash and herbs and surround them with native flowering plants, it is more likely that the hornworm will be discovered by the parasitic and beneficial wasp that uses the hornworm's body as a host for its larva and will, in turn, hatch more of these beneficial wasps. If nothing else, practicing biodiversity in this garden can lessen the amount of damage caused, limiting the hornworm to the single tomato plant rather than the buffet of a whole row planted together.

Birds on Pest Patrol

Birds are at the top of the soil food web and are a vital, and often missing, key to balancing the ecosystem and creating a healthy garden—by helping to reduce the number of insects damaging your plants.

Sadly, bird populations are in a global decline, a result of a diminishing number of insects that feed young birds and the effects of changing global temperatures that create a reduction in habitat. As of 2023, around half of the world's 10,000 bird species are in decline, and 1 in 8 faces extinction. This downturn has been seen over the last several decades, and the numbers are startling and sobering: A quarter of US bird life has disappeared in just the past 50 years.

This is inherently tied to the performance of the garden. When birds, as the top of the food chain, are missing from our gardens, many bugs can proliferate unchecked. Birds help regulate ecosystems by consuming insects (including squash bugs, squash vine borers, earwigs, hornworms, and cabbage moths), spreading seeds, and pollinating plants. They are a key piece of the healthy garden (and planet) ecosystem.

A thicket of American plums, chokecherries, and golden currants provides nesting habitat for birds as well as a perpetual and preferred food source.

Robins make a home on the barn at the edge of the field.

SQUASH VINE BORER AS FOOD FOR BIRDS

Biodiversity can help with many other frequent "pests" in the garden. Take the squash vine borer, an insect that burrows into the vining part of squash and pumpkins. An infestation of these borers can make a harvest of watermelon, squash, cucumbers, and pumpkins nearly impossible.

The common organic recommendations for dealing with squash vine borers include *Bacillus thuringiensis* subsp. *kurstaki* (*Btk*), which gets sprayed on plants and will kill caterpillars that feed on the vines or leaves of the plant. Misapplication of this pesticide, including allowing it to drift onto surrounding plants, can kill nontarget insects such as swallowtail and monarch caterpillars and can also reduce the caterpillar food source that is key for attracting birds to the garden. (Birds primarily feed caterpillars to their young; a study by Dr. Douglas Tallamy indicates that chickadees feed their babies 350 to 570 caterpillars each day, or 6,000 to 9,000 caterpillars for one family of birds!) Toads, bats, frogs, and other insects also feed on caterpillars.

New research also indicates that *Bacillus thuringiensis*—in particular, new subspecies of it—affects more than just the targeted insects, and external effects can trigger consequences throughout the ecosystem, especially when it's applied repeatedly.

By spraying these plants to kill off leaf-eating caterpillars, we are ignoring the food source needs of the biodiverse ecosystem of the garden. Additionally, due to the overuse of *Btk*, some strains of moths are now exhibiting resistance.

APHIDS FEED BENEFICIAL INSECTS

Almost every gardener has dealt with this common garden nemesis. Aphids suck the life from plants, enjoying their rapid green growth, and can kill plants in great numbers, leading most gardeners to take action early upon seeing them.

Neem oil is a commonly recommended organic remedy for aphids. Derived from the neem tree, it is considered natural by many and therefore has the connotation of being safe. But contrary to this understanding, neem is an indiscriminate killer and will kill all soft-bodied insects that come into contact with it. This means that

The aphids on the lower leaf will provide sustenance for the beneficial green lacewing above.

any beneficial insects starting to move in to protect the plant from aphid damage—such as lacewings, ladybugs, spiders, or aphid midges—will also be wiped out, eliminating nature's system of balance that would support aphid control. If we simply exercise patience with aphids and support a biodiverse ecosystem that includes native plants, the beneficial insects will move in and devour the tiny aphids—it is incredible to watch. When we consider the ecosystem of the garden, this makes sense. Aphids are the food source for many beneficial and helpful garden bugs. Without this food source, the protectors will not come to our aid!

Understanding Biodiversity Beyond the Garden

Keep in mind that the garden ecosystem does not stop at the boundary of the raised bed or vegetable growing area; it's not an island. Not only do we often see monocultures in the home production garden, we also see them in the landscape around the garden—which is almost as important as the garden itself! The backyard, the "hellstrip" (that piece of land between the sidewalk and the street), the landscaping around the front door, and the dead zone in the alley can all be put to work to increase the biodiversity of the garden.

A robin searches for caterpillars for its young under a peony plant edged with native blue grama grass.

How to Deal with Pests in the Regenerative Garden

One of the questions I'm asked the most often is, "How do you deal with this pest in the garden?" I typically give the same response: What is missing in your ecosystem? Are the bugs doing actual damage, or are they just bothering and worrying you? If the latter, take 10 steps back from the garden and try to relax and let nature do its thing. If the former, first give it some time. If you're following the planting recommendations of this book and including a diverse range of native plants around the garden, wait and see if predator insects begin to appear to manage the problem bug at hand. If none arrive, start with manual options first: handpicking, insect netting, an empty tuna can with a dash of soy sauce or beer and vegetable oil. Pay attention to your soil—unhealthy soil is often the root cause of many pest issues, creating plants that lack vigor, are fertilizer dependent, and are vulnerable to predation.

Create Habitat with Native Plants

To understand why native plants specifically are vital to this discussion, we first need to recognize that ecosystems are delicately balanced and regionally specific. The insects native to an ecoregion, and key to ecosystem balance, have evolved over thousands of years to use certain plants for nectar and as reproduction hosts. In many cases, their survival and ability to thrive hinge on the right plants being available.

THE PLANT-POLLINATOR RELATIONSHIP

The honeybee was originally brought to the US from Europe and is considered a generalist pollinator, feeding on any pollen-producing plant. In contrast, many of our vital native specialist pollinators—which make up between 19 and 37 percent of native bee species—will feed and reproduce only on a few specific plants. This makes them particularly vulnerable to habitat loss.

A leaf-cutter bee has used this milkweed leaf for habitat construction.

A swallowtail butterfly feeds on the nectar of the native Rocky Mountain penstemon plant at the farm.

Native swallowtail caterpillars have evolved to feed on nonnative fennel.

Bumblebees are superior pollinators to the European honeybee, so attracting them will help with fruit production in the garden. Here, one feeds on native bee balm.

One of the best and most well-known examples of a specialist pollinator is the monarch butterfly, which doesn't just prefer but requires plants from the *Asclepias* genus (milkweed) to reproduce—their larvae are only able to consume and survive on that plant. Life for these specialist insects is risky and difficult. As native plants disappear from landscapes and natural areas, their vital forage becomes fewer and farther between, and their populations dwindle. As the diversity of native plants shrinks, so do the populations of native insects, and with them, the ecosystem balance in the garden.

Some of the best plants for native specialist pollinators in North America include those in the family Asteraceae (such as asters, rudbeckias, sunflowers, and goldenrods), which provide nectar and pollen for a number of specialists.

NATIVE PLANTS ARE WELL ADAPTED TO THEIR ENVIRONMENT

Native plants not only attract a diverse range of insects to the garden, they are also easier to maintain. Because they prefer the climate of the ecoregion they evolved in, they typically don't require soil amendments, additional fertilizers, or additional water (though many will still appreciate it in drought years). Many native plants do have a tendency to become large or spread rapidly, so be mindful of their placement within the landscape. Native plants are incredible as part of a garden, but planting them in the wrong location could make you resent them!

Thistles were one of many monocultures that had to be cleared before we could establish a vibrant ecosystem.

Avoid Planting Invasive Plants

Invasive plants often lead to decreased biodiversity. Invasive plants are any nonnative plant that spreads aggressively at the expense of native plants. In many cases, invasive plants not only spread so rapidly that they choke out valuable native plants, but they can even change the soil chemistry to be less hospitable to those native plants. This results in an ecosystem that fails to attract native beneficial insects and will quickly become unbalanced as the ecosystem becomes less favorable to biodiversity and turns instead toward a monoculture.

It can be difficult to tell which plants are invasive, especially because they are commonly sold at garden centers, both as plants and as seeds—including English ivy, butterfly bush, burning bush, dame's rocket, sweet alyssum, and Queen Anne's lace. The horticultural industry has done a massive amount of damage to the ecosystems of North America by introducing such plants, either as "exotic" ornamentals or for erosion control. For example, the kudzu vine, which was showcased at the 1876 Centennial Exposition in Philadelphia and praised for its rapid, sturdy growth and sweet-smelling blooms, is now decimating entire forests. Similarly, the damaging multiflora rose was originally offered as a hedge plant to slow erosion.

Beyond the fact that they often serve little purpose for our native beneficials and wildlife, invasives skew the entire ecosystem to be less attractive for the native beneficial insects that serve as warriors in the garden; and, over time, invasive plants will spread out of control. (See What Are Invasive Plants? on page 135.)

Healthy Soil Supports a Healthy Ecosystem

Soil that is properly balanced will provide the right nutrients for the ecosystem's organisms. From the bottom rung of the soil food web up to the top, soil is the cornerstone of the thriving garden ecosystem. Rich in nutrients, beneficial microbes, and organic matter, healthy garden soil supplies the essential foundation for plant growth and vitality and hosts a diverse community of organisms to cycle nutrients and improve soil structure.

On the other hand, excess fertilizer often leads to sick soils and the death of soil microbes, fungi, and the vital symbiosis between plant roots and soil life. Creating soil that is vigorous and healthy involves feeding the soil food web (see Chapter 2). Every consideration and decision made in the garden should center around how it affects the health of the soil. Nurturing the soil will not only foster robust plant growth but also enhance the overall ecosystem resilience in the garden.

A handful of topsoil contains a healthy amount of organic matter to provide a food source for the soil food web.

Guerrilla Gardening, Anyone?

Growing on a smaller scale? Even if your garden is small or limited to a balcony, you, too, can create an ecosystem! Most landscaping, especially commercial landscaping, lacks native plants and the diversity of plantings needed to facilitate a healthy ecosystem of beneficials. But don't despair! Not only can you find smaller native plants (and cultivars bred to be more friendly in urban landscapes) that thrive in patio spaces while serving the ecosystem and attracting beneficials, you could also consider going beyond your own space.

Is there an unclaimed alley behind your home that has become overgrown with weeds where you could toss some native seeds or tend the space without anyone minding? (Be sure not to plant anything with deep roots that could disturb foundations or infrastructure.) Perhaps a neighbor who doesn't use their yard wouldn't mind you planting some bird-attracting plants in their space. Look beyond your own garden and your own property to supplement your garden ecosystem, and think in a community-minded way.

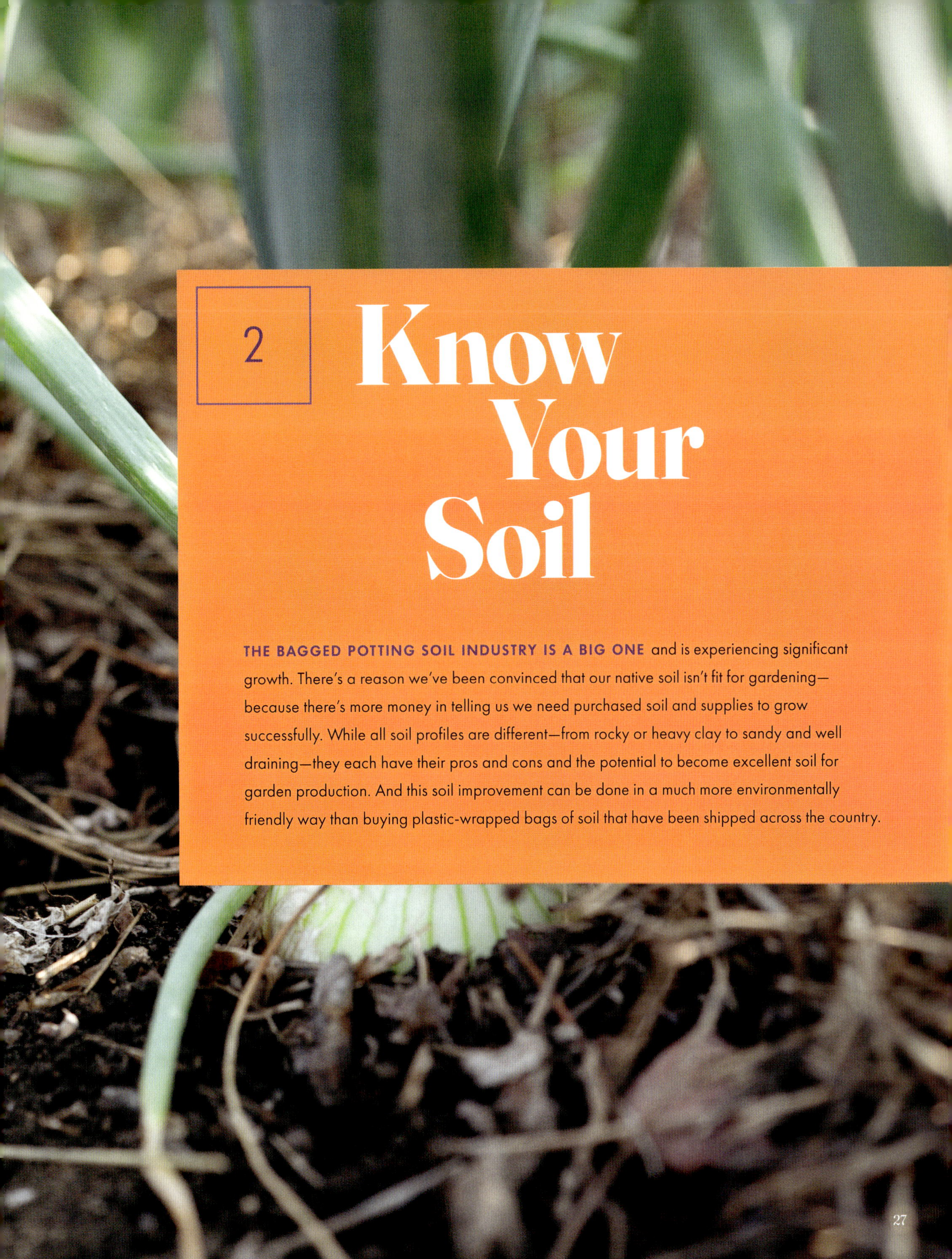

2

Know Your Soil

THE BAGGED POTTING SOIL INDUSTRY IS A BIG ONE and is experiencing significant growth. There's a reason we've been convinced that our native soil isn't fit for gardening—because there's more money in telling us we need purchased soil and supplies to grow successfully. While all soil profiles are different—from rocky or heavy clay to sandy and well draining—they each have their pros and cons and the potential to become excellent soil for garden production. And this soil improvement can be done in a much more environmentally friendly way than buying plastic-wrapped bags of soil that have been shipped across the country.

Once heavy clay, this soil was transformed into a thriving garden with just a few simple, budget-friendly tweaks, like using cover cropping and organic mulches.

Learn to Read Your Soil

There is a lot to be learned about soil through a simple visual and physical examination. While much of what is happening beneath the soil is invisible to the naked eye, just as much information that can inform our practices is right at our fingertips.

The first time I started a garden, I headed to the garden center, bought a few bags of the best soil I could afford to fill the raised bed my husband had built in the backyard, and planted into it. As it turned out, I hadn't exactly budgeted enough space (gardeners can relate—there is *never* enough space), so we created a makeshift second garden in our native soil by digging out the grass and surrounding the area with bricks. The bed was just meant to be an overflow; I popped some of my extra tomato and pepper plants in it after the main bed was full, expecting to get a little produce but for the raised bed filled with the purchased soil to be the better producer. And I'll be darned—that secondary garden bed outperformed the nice raised container filled with the expensive purchased material.

Had I taken the time to do a basic soil test and physical examination of my soil, I could have saved myself a lot of money and effort. Inspecting the soil would have shown me that while it was heavy, it had a sweet, earthy smell; was slightly crumbly; held moisture well; and contained a handful of worms in each shovelful—all indicators of good soil health. Even simple observations can lead us to major insights about our soil's condition and how to improve it for gardening.

Touch It

Determine the soil texture (the relative proportions of sand, silt, and clay particles in soil). Pick up a handful of moist soil. (If it isn't moist, dampen it lightly—but not to the point of being soaked.) Roll and squeeze it into a ball with your hand.

Clayey. Does it hold together like a piece of clay and become difficult to break apart? If so, your soil has a heavy clay content. Clay soil typically contains more than 40 percent clay and is sticky when wet. Although it can retain water and nutrients well, it can drain poorly, leading to waterlogged plants and rotting roots. A clay soil will benefit from the addition of organic matter to create aeration and drainage.

This loamy soil has a balance of different-size particles and some organic matter mixed in.

TESTING FOR COMPACTION

Remove the round bottom pan from a springform pan so just the ring remains. Press the ring to a depth of about 3 inches.

Fill the ring with water.

Let drain until no water remains but the soil is still glistening. Healthy soil drains at a rate of 1 to 2 inches per hour.

Sandy. Does the soil not hold a ball at all, and are sand particles visible? If so, your soil has a high sand content. The particles of sandy soil are coarse, creating loose soil that drains quickly, making it poor at retaining water and nutrients. Sandy soils will cool and heat more rapidly than clayey soils of the same color, resulting in more rapid temperature fluctuations. Sandy soil also will appreciate organic matter, which helps retain nutrients and moisture in the soil.

Silty. Silt particles are smoother and finer than sand but larger than clay, making silty soil retain water better than sandy soil but drain more easily than clay. Silty soils tend to be fertile but can compact easily, leading to issues with aeration. Organic matter and plant roots in the soil will help reduce the risk of compaction.

Loamy/Balanced. If the ball forms small clumps but still crumbles apart, it has a good balance of sand, clay, silt, and other organic matter particles that form soil aggregates—the key to good soil structure. You'll notice that each soil type benefits from the addition of organic matter for different reasons, regardless of structure.

Try inserting a wire flag (the kind used to mark out utilities and irrigation lines) into soil that is moist but not saturated. Hold the wire at the flag end and push it into the soil until it begins to bend. If the wire penetrates to a depth of about 8 inches or more, the soil is considered not compacted. That's good! If the wire goes less than 4 inches into the soil, the soil is considered moderately compacted.

Many plants struggle to grow in compacted soil. Soil compaction occurs due to traffic (walking or driving on the surface) and/or a lack of organic matter and soil life. An active soil food web creates aeration, which results in a spongier soil. Compacted soil often has high clay content and would benefit from the addition of organic matter and the presence of living plant roots.

Another way to gauge soil compaction is by measuring the water infiltration rate. To check this, I use a round cake pan with a removable (and thus not watertight) bottom, like a springform pan. Remove the bottom and press the ring down into the soil about halfway and fill it with water. Notice how quickly or slowly the water seeps out and infiltrates the soil surface. Healthy soil drains water at a rate of 1 to 2 inches per hour. Slower infiltration indicates compacted soil or a high clay content. Very rapid infiltration potentially indicates sandy soils that could benefit from organic matter and plant roots to slow the rate of drainage.

Look at It

Visually examine the soil surface. What is the soil's color and overall appearance?

Light color. Sandier soils are often lighter in color. Lighter colors might also indicate mineral content; for example, soils high in calcium carbonate or lime can have a whitish hue, whereas those high in iron can appear reddish. While soil doesn't necessarily have to be dark to be healthy, very light color in soil may indicate a lack of organic matter.

Dark color. Darker soils may indicate higher levels of organic matter and also moisture. If your soil stays darker for a while after rain or watering, it may have a high content of clay, which tends to retain moisture.

Cracking. Cracked soil is not uncommon and is often seen in areas where soil protection and organic matter are lacking. Cracking indicates a dry-wet pattern detrimental to soil life (common in clay soil), and the soil would likely benefit from a layer of mulch to protect the microbes from fluctuations in moisture and temperature.

Smell It

Yes, smell your soil! There's nothing like olfactory cues to help tell you the state of your soil, particularly when it pertains to drainage. Dig down a few inches and scoop up a shovelful. Get your nose close to the scoop and inhale deeply!

Light soil can lack the organic matter needed to support the soil food web.

Cracking often signifies compacted clay soil.

Dark, rich soil contains organic matter that retains moisture and nutrients.

Soil smells sweet. Soil should have a slightly sweet, organic scent, like how the earth smells after a gentle rain in spring.

Soil smells sour or rotten. Similar to the scent of an unturned compost pile, soil can sometimes smell sour, like decomposing food. This is common with clayey soils and indicates anaerobic, or oxygen-depleted, conditions, caused by a lack of organic matter or larger soil aggregates that help oxygenate soil and provide spaces for aerobic soil life to survive. Sour-smelling soil will often be compacted.

Unpleasant-smelling soil can be remedied through the long-term addition of organic matter via cover crops or mulch (are we picking up a theme yet?)—and in the short term through the use of a broadfork, a pitchforklike tool with wide tines, to lightly aerate soil without turning it and disturbing any existing soil life.

This rose is starting to show a light green appearance on its older growth, an early sign of nitrogen deficiency (or possibly overwatering).

Check for Indicators of Plant Health

Many indicators of plant health appear right in front of our eyes as our garden grows during the season.

Pale plant growth. Are the older, lower leaves turning yellow while younger leaves remain green? Do the stems appear spindly and leaves look small and stunted? This may indicate a nitrogen deficiency. Try adding alfalfa pellet fertilizer (for edible plants) or manure tea (for ornamental plants) for a short-term boost. Add a nitrogen-fixing cover crop as part of long term nutrient management. Some other issues, like overwatering or iron deficiency, can also present as light yellow growth, so checking soil moisture and getting a soil test are also helpful in identifying whether any nutrients are out of balance.

Plants that are too leafy. Are plants overly leafy and growing quickly, and are there lots of aphids in the garden? It's possible to have *too much* nitrogen, which results in rapid new growth attractive to sucking pests like aphids. Perhaps excess nitrogen has been applied to the soil through fertilizers or composted manure applications.

Rapid new growth on a bolted radish attracts aphids—also note the faint outline of brown lacewings, a primary aphid predator.

Investigate Further

Check your soil for signs of ecosystem health.

Rocks, chunks, and organic debris. Expect to find rocks and small chunks of organic matter like leaves, straw, plant debris, and sticks in your soil. While a few larger pieces of organic matter don't create an issue, working a lot of larger wood chips (greater than approximately 2 inches in diameter) into the soil, for example, can create nitrogen deficiencies as that matter gets broken down. That's because microbes require nitrogen to decompose the carbon-rich wood chips, which in turn can reduce the availability of nitrogen for plant uptake and thus stunt plant growth and vitality. It's okay to place wood chips on *top* of the soil, but you don't want to mix them in around plant roots.

Rocks can be more beneficial than you might think—they break down slowly into minerals and help aerate the soil by creating air pockets. Very large rocks, of course, impede root development, but rocky soil is not a major problem in and of itself.

Visually inspect soil health in your beds by checking for rocks, organic matter, and living worms, insects, and other organisms.

Dig up a full shovelful of soil after clearing away wood chip mulch in order to see what's happening below the surface.

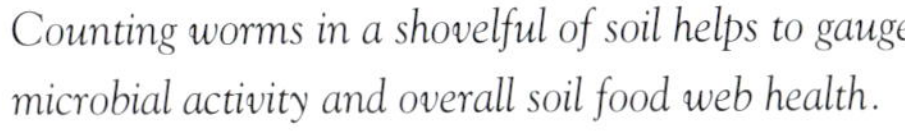

Counting worms in a shovelful of soil helps to gauge microbial activity and overall soil food web health.

This Rocky Mountain bee plant has damage from flea beetles. Fortunately, ladybugs moved in to balance their population.

Worms, insects, and bugs. Does a visual examination of the soil reveal a variety of insect life? The presence of life within our soil can be an excellent sign of health. Seeing worms (or wormholes), various decomposers like pill bugs, and other beetles, spiders, ground nesting bees, and more signals a healthy and balanced garden soil ecosystem.

On the other hand, indications of poor soil health can be seen through the bug damage on plants: A proliferation of one type of garden pest can indicate a deeper issue within the soil food web. For instance, excess fertilizer use can be detrimental to the health of the soil microbes and therefore also affect the complicated relationship plants form with the soil around the root zone.

If plants are being decimated by pests, you will notice that those plants may lack health and vigor—healthy plants are better able to thwart nibblers, both by becoming more difficult for pests to eat and through the fascinating relationship plants form with soil microbes. If plants are unable to resist pests, it is likely that the garden's ecosystem is not yet balanced.

Although we will list some helpful solutions to balancing the garden ecosystem in the recipe section of the book (see page 183), remember that regenerative gardening is not a quick fix but a gentle healing process. To better understand this, let's review a key element of the health of the garden: the soil food web.

What Do Weeds Signal in the Garden?

Step back and look at the area as a whole—is there a great deal of one type of weed? While there is anecdotal evidence that the presence of certain weeds gives us information about soil conditions, not all of these anecdotes are true. For example, burdock, a deep taproot–creating weed, is thought to grow in compacted soil, even though we know that burdock actually prefers sandy and well-draining soil. Plantain allegedly indicates more acidic soils, yet on our farm, we have a fair amount of it, and our soil is quite alkaline.

This doesn't mean that weeds can't be helpful; for example, taproot weeds like burdock and dandelion can function similarly to a cover crop of radish, helping to aerate and break up heavy soil. So while weeds can serve a purpose, it can be difficult to use them as an indicator of what is happening in the soil. A sandy, well-draining, acidic soil is just as likely to contain dandelions as a clayey, compacted, alkaline soil, given enough dandelion seeds floating around! Often, weeds simply signal that there is a heavy weed seed bank or an active population of invasive weeds in your area, and that your soil has bare spots that those weed seeds are able to take advantage of as nature fills the void. Yes, it can be helpful to evaluate and track weed types, but don't base your soil evaluation solely on which weeds exist in the space, or you might be misled.

While weeds can sometimes indicate certain soil conditions such as compaction, they are often simply a symptom of a large weed seed bank or noxious weeds in the area. Due to their underground creep, rhizome-based weeds (left) are more difficult to control than taproot-based weeds (right).

Getting to Know the Soil Food Web

To understand the garden and how the soil within it functions as a part of the ecosystem, we first need a basic understanding of what is happening beneath our feet—and this begins with the soil food web. The health of the soil food web is vital to the vigor not only of our plants but also of our gardens, our neighborhood ecosystem, and the planet as a whole. Gaps or holes in the soil food web, as in any ecosystem, can lead to bigger issues up the food chain, such as the decline of bird activity in the garden. On a planetary scale, without the soil food web, human life would cease to exist.

The soil food web is an example of the intricate relationships between microbes, fungi, insects, plant roots, and animals that sustain a healthy, living soil ecosystem.

The Four Components of the Soil Food Web

Just what is the soil food web? It's the complicated interwoven interactions between arthropods, microbes, fungi, bacteria, worms, and small animals. Each component, or layer, is important to the function and performance of plants, from making nutrients available via the decomposition of organic matter to enhancing a plant's ability to ward off insect damage (see Soil Health and Preventing Insect Damage, page 40). The soil food web is a bustling community of organisms, and each plays important roles in maintaining soil health. Although the soil food web is a complicated system, having even a basic appreciation of it is sufficient for understanding its effects in the garden.

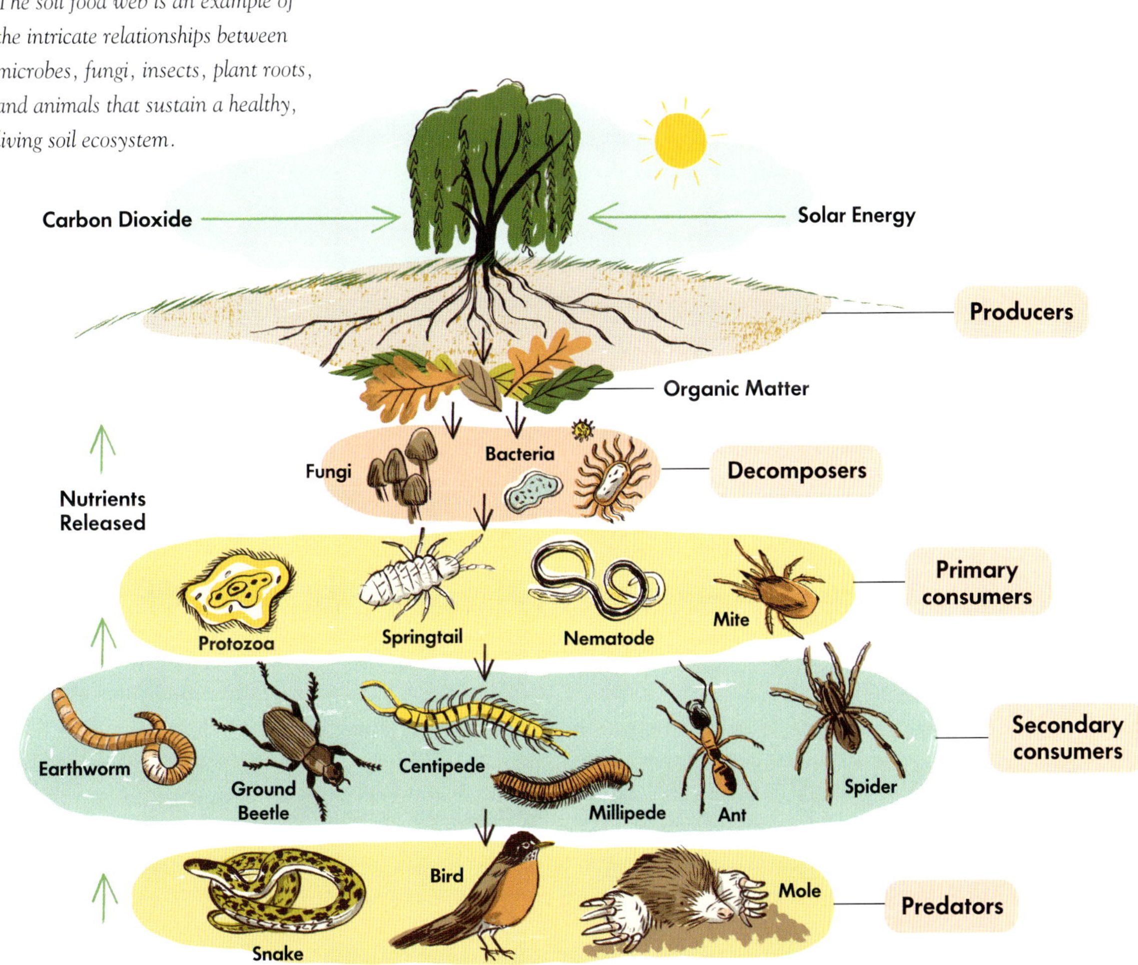

An earthworm is intertwined with these roots. Worms frequently are found around plant roots, where they consume the smaller members of the soil food web often present there.

White growth on soil indicates fungal mycelium in soil.

THE PRODUCERS

The first layer of the soil food web consists of the producers: the photosynthesizing plants, such as grasses, trees, and garden plants, and their roots. The most important part of any food web is its lowest rung. In the case of the soil food web, this layer is made up of the plant roots; remember this for later! The food web starts with the plants that photosynthesize energy from the sun and pull carbon dioxide from the atmosphere down into the soil via their roots. These roots begin the process of building organic matter in the soil. Also within this layer are dead plant roots, dead bugs, and other decaying matter, such as rocks, that add carbon and minerals to the soil. Think of the producers as the foundation of the soil food web, providing energy to everything else.

THE DECOMPOSERS

That organic matter becomes food for the next layer of the food web—the decomposers, including bacteria, fungi, small insects, and other organisms such as earthworms. These organisms break down dead plant material like roots and fallen leaves and turn it into nutrient-rich organic matter. They are tough to visualize—there are literally millions of these organisms in a handful of soil! Much of this soil life layer forms a symbiotic relationship with plants. The plant roots feed the fungi, and the fungi, in exchange, form a mycorrhizal network of threads that help the plant take up nutrients and water.

In a typical healthy interaction between plants and soil, as the plant photosynthesizes sunlight and fixes atmospheric carbon dioxide, its roots release exudates (sugars, along with some protein and carbohydrates). These become food for rhizobia, microbes surrounding the plant roots in an area called the rhizosphere. Each plant releases its own unique blend of exudates to attract the rhizobia and mycorrhizal fungi that it needs. In exchange, the microbes mineralize the existing nutrients in the soil (from things like rocks, grains of sand, plant matter, and dead insects) and provide them in a plant-available form to the roots.

Other members of this food web level include pathogens, parasites, and root feeders, and all thrive along with bacteria and fungi in the root area of the plant. The dark organic matter produced by these decomposers is what improves

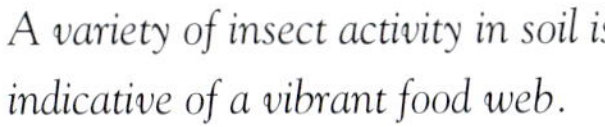

A variety of insect activity in soil is indicative of a vibrant food web.

While not technically part of the soil, small mammals and birds are also vital to the performance of the garden.

soil fertility and structure and provides food for other organisms.

THE CONSUMERS

In the soil food web, large consumers play a vital role in maintaining the balance of soil ecosystems. These creatures, which include larger insects like beetles, millipedes, and spiders, are key predators, feeding on smaller insects and controlling their populations. Furthermore, the presence of insects aids in soil aeration and mixing, enhancing soil structure, promoting better nutrient distribution, and ultimately fostering healthier and more productive soils.

Earthworms, which serve as decomposers (see facing page), also play a role in this phase of the soil food web. They contribute to nutrient cycling by feeding on decomposing organic matter and microorganisms such as soil bacteria within the rhizosphere. This interaction explains why, when we disturb the soil around plants during planting or gardening, we often encounter a plethora of earthworms actively feeding on the rich microbial life within the roots.

THE PREDATORS

The predators are animals like birds, toads and frogs, moles, and some insects that eat the consumer organisms. They help control the populations of pests and keep the soil ecosystem in balance. Birds are an incredibly vital part of the soil food web. They are frequently forgotten or considered a nuisance in the garden, snacking on berries and poking holes in our tomatoes—but they are actually *essential* to healthy control of the larger arthropods that can be problematic when their populations boom.

At the top of the soil food web are higher-level predators. These larger animals—like foxes, snakes, and birds of prey—feed on and help regulate the populations of smaller predators, ensuring that the soil ecosystem remains stable.

A rabbit munches on a garden bed planted with a cover crop of oats and peas, fertilizing the garden with its manure and serving as a food source for hawks and owls. Golden currants in the background provide bird habitat.

Maintaining a Healthy Soil Food Web

The soil food web is a complex network wherein energy and nutrients flow from the bottom-level producers (plant roots) and up through each level of the food web. Plants photosynthesize and produce sugars and other compounds, which they exude through their roots. These serve as a source of food and energy for the other members of the soil food web that, in turn, break down organic matter and convert nutrients into forms accessible to plants, thus facilitating nutrient uptake.

Each group of organisms has its own unique role in breaking down organic matter, cycling nutrients, and maintaining overall soil health. When all levels work together, they create fertile soil that supports the health of the plants that, in turn, sustain the whole ecosystem of the garden.

The key is to remember the butterfly effect: Every small action taken with the soil can affect a component of the food web that can affect the ecosystem of the soil as well as the outcome of your garden. Treating the soil gently and with reverence for the billions of lives within it is an important part of creating and sustaining a regenerative garden.

Frenemies, Not Enemies

Although we often think of insects in our gardens as enemies, it's clear from a study of the soil food web that each insect has an important role to play in the soil ecosystem. The caterpillars (yes, including the dreaded hornworm) that we occasionally find feeding on our plants and try to eliminate are vital food for one of the most important levels of the soil food web: the birds. Birds rely on these caterpillars as a main source of food for their young.

Don't Flip Your Soil Layers

Another concept to consider when discussing the soil food web is whether the soil life is aerobic or anaerobic—that is, does it thrive in the presence or absence of oxygen? In the layers of the soil food web closer to the surface, soil life needs oxygen. This is why having aeration in the upper soil levels is beneficial!

In the deeper, more compacted layers of the soil, soil life skews more toward the anaerobic side, not needing as much oxygen. This is one reason why overworking and turning the soil can be detrimental to soil microorganisms: By bringing deeper layers to the surface and moving surface layers downward, we expose anaerobic layers to oxygen and UV rays as we push aerobic layers down too deeply, where they will suffocate, and we destroy the structure that allows aerobic microbes to thrive.

Many aerobic organisms living on the soil surface, such as ants, beetles, and spiders, interact with both the soil and the aboveground environment. They require oxygen to survive.

Creatures that move between the surface and the soil, like springtails and some insect larvae, play key roles in decomposition and nutrient cycling.

Soil-dwellers that live entirely below the surface, including earthworms, nematodes, and microbes, are essential for soil structure, fertility, and long-term ecosystem health.

When we try to eliminate insect nibblers, either via pesticides or manual removal, we interfere with the soil food web, making our gardens less hospitable to the birds who play a valuable role in keeping populations of potentially damaging insects under control. If, on the other hand, we focus on supporting and attracting birds to our garden, we'll see a reduction in the "pest" pressures many of us are desperate to correct.

A chickadee brings an insect to its young, helping maintain balance in the garden.

Soil Health and Preventing Insect Damage

One of the most interesting aspects of soil life is the interaction between the plants and microbes when insects are damaging the plants. Research has found that when a plant is nibbled on, it produces a series of chemical responses to attract the beneficial insects that will help ward off the attacker. Through its root exudates (see page 36), a plant signals to soil microbes that it needs assistance in fighting off the damaging organisms. The microbes, in turn, provide the plant with the nutrients it needs to send out a type of "bat signal" to the beneficial insects that will help ward off the attack.

We can see this process in action when aphids appear in the garden. We often leap to a plant's defense when we see aphids swarming, but if we instead leave the plant to its own defenses, the plant sends signals to beneficials like lacewings and ladybugs, that then begin to move in on their own to eat the aphids. While there may be some losses from the damage that occurs in the meantime, once the beneficials become established in the garden, they will continue to protect against future aphid outbreaks and minimize overall damage, making the garden require less hands-on labor in the long term.

We gardeners are still learning about these complex interactions, but we do know that it is much more complex than we currently understand, and we know that human interference—such as the application of fertilizers and pesticides—can often negatively affect these communications between plants and microorganisms within the soil.

The lacewing eggs hanging off the leaf of this milkweed plant are about to hatch. When they do, they will feed on the aphids now covering the plant, bringing them in check.

These queens of the garden, Café au Lait dahlias, no longer need to be covered with protective bags, thanks to practices that foster biodiversity and nearby native plants.

How to Minimize Negative Effects on the Soil Food Web

Gardeners can inadvertently damage the soil food web, with lasting detrimental effects on the garden ecosystem. The good news is, with mindful practices, we can also protect and nurture this vital underground network. Here's how.

Avoid Applying Unnecessary Fertilizers

The more fertilizers we add to the soil to hasten plant growth, the more they reduce the proper functioning of the soil food web. Looking at the producers level of the soil food web helps us understand why. Plant roots put out a unique blend of root exudates that attract a specific mix of rhizospheric bacteria favorable for plant growth and productivity. When we interfere with this process, the plant puts out fewer of these root exudates and attracts fewer of the soil microbes it will need later to ward off insect attacks and grow more resiliently.

It is completely normal for plant growth to be slightly slower in spring and for soil life to become more active as soil temperatures warm. But gardeners, impatient from cold winters and anxious for full, green plants, often apply excess nitrogen growth fertilizers to the soil early in the season. While this may achieve lush green growth, it also generates "lazy" plants (and attracts those hordes of aphids)! When a plant receives nitrogen and other nutrients from fertilizers, it doesn't send out root exudates, because the plant is already receiving the nutrients it would otherwise receive from the microorganism interaction in the rhizosphere. This creates a cycle of dependence on fertilizers: Once plants have utilized the fertilizer nutrients, growth slows because the plants are unable to get more nutrients from the soil, not having formed the necessary reciprocal relationship with the soil life. In effect, we create plants that are addicted to fertilizer and are more sensitive to pest damage.

Bloom fertilizers, which are often high in soluble phosphates, can have negative effects on the soil food web by prohibiting the growth of mycorrhizal fungi that form extensive networks of fungal hyphae strands between plant roots and the soil to enable the plant to seek nutrients from farther out in the soil. Research has shown that when soluble phosphate levels (soluble being the type applied in fertilizer form) are above 10 parts per million (a relatively small number), mycorrhizal growth is hindered. So while the plants may experience a burst of rapid nutrient uptake from fertilizer amendments, it is at the expense of the sustaining associations with the soil food web that would otherwise create healthier plants that don't need outside amendments. Lacking these vital alliances can make plants more vulnerable to both nutrient deficiencies and pest attacks.

Avoid Tilling/Disturbing the Soil Whenever Possible

Disturbing the soil has detrimental effects on soil aggregation, in addition to disrupting the anaerobic and aerobic layers of soil life (see page 39). Tilling and turning the soil trigger bacterial activity that will rapidly consume the soil's existing organic matter, quickly depleting this source of energy while releasing carbon dioxide into the atmosphere and hastening global climate change. The aggressive impact of working the soil can also kill many of the nematodes, fungal strands, arthropods, and other organisms living there. And while the soil food web can be regrown, it takes time to do so. We may utilize tilling one time to establish a new bed, but frequent tilling or turning the garden as part of regular maintenance will damage soil and plant health.

Working the soil also causes erosion, and tilling is as detrimental to home garden topsoil

A broadfork gently cracks the soil to aerate a garden bed.

as it is to soil on a large-scale farm. Since farmers began tilling the North American midwestern prairies 160 years ago, it's estimated that around 57.6 billion metric tons of topsoil have eroded from the once-fertile earth, the nutrients needed to grow food gone along with it. Remnants of native prairie are around 1.2 feet higher than farmed soils on average, a shocking number, as it takes about 1,000 years to rebuild 1 inch of topsoil. According to United Nations officials in the Food and Agriculture Organization, there are only approximately 60 seasons of harvests remaining in global existing topsoil. These losses are mostly due to intensive farming practices, not those of home gardening, but they illustrate how much soil erosion takes place because of poor soil conservation practices and repeated tilling. Instead, if the soil in a home garden needs aeration after establishment, I recommend utilizing a lower-disturbance method such as broadforking (see page 162) to gently work air into the soil without creating excessive disturbance.

Avoid Applying Pesticides

Thousands of pest products are sold with the message that gardening success depends on them. Some are organic, while others are more nefarious and systemic (such as the neonicotinoid imidacloprid) and can reside in the genetics of the plants for years to come, contaminating leaves and pollen and killing pollinators and other insects that feed on the plants. These pesticides work by translocation; that is, pesticide that is applied to any part of the plant can migrate via the xylem and phloem to other parts of the plant, such as the pollen and nectar. A systemic pesticide applied to the leaves or soil around roses to target Japanese beetles, for example, has the potential to migrate to the pollen and nectar of the plant and be taken up by foraging honeybees and other pollinators. And the effect isn't limited to the aboveground ecosystems that we can see: Pesticides also have negative effects on soil microbes.

A study published in *Scientific American* in 2021 illustrates how pesticides affect soil microbiology. Researchers at the Center for Biological Diversity, Friends of the Earth, and the University of Maryland analyzed nearly 400 published studies, which were based on more than 2,800 experiments on the effect pesticide applications have on soil organisms. The results were clear. In over 70 percent of the experiments, the pesticides harmed the soil organisms, not just the target pests. The Food and Agriculture Organization of the United Nations has identified pesticide-intensive agriculture as the most significant contributor to the loss of soil biodiversity over the last decade.

PESTICIDES KILL MORE THAN JUST TARGETED INSECTS

The biggest issue with pesticides is that, more often than not, they are not as targeted as they claim to be. If our gardens are being inundated with aphids, earwigs, or Japanese beetles, we might intend to apply a single pesticide that will target only the insect we are concerned with, while protecting the bees, butterfly caterpillars, and beneficial insects key to the healthy survival of the ecosystem. Unfortunately, this is not the result—spraying products that seem innocuous can hurt beneficial insects as well as "pests."

A bumblebee rests at dusk on the underside of a lavender flower, vulnerable to dusk-applied pesticides.

Neem. Neem oil is touted as safe and organic, but the truth is that neem is actually a broad-spectrum contact pesticide. At rates recommended for use as a pesticide in the garden, it will kill bees, spiders, and soft-bodied insects by clogging their respiratory systems, resulting in suffocation. The University of California lists neem oil as being "moderately toxic" to bees, recommending that it be applied only at times when "pollinators are not active." The problem with this is that many pollinators, such as North American native bumblebees, often rest on the underside of blooms at night, making them vulnerable to dusk applications. Azadirachtin, the active ingredient in neem oil, is a powerful insect growth disruptor, and pollinators feeding on impacted pollen can see reduced larval populations, hindering the production of future generations. The azadirachtin also works as an antifeedant, and leaves of plants treated with neem that are fed on by caterpillars (such as those of monarchs) can cause those important insects to stop eating and starve.

Diatomaceous earth. Also referred to as DE, this oft-recommended "natural" pesticide is made of the fossilized skeletons of microscopic single-celled aquatic organisms (mined from marine deposits in the western United States). This sharp-edged material cuts the bodies of insects and leads to dehydration. Although it's effective against slugs and snails and even aphids, it is indiscriminate and will also kill ladybugs, lacewings, and spiders.

In short, there is no magical formula that will protect beneficial insects from the effects of pesticides. The overall effect of using pesticides extends throughout the garden ecosystem and can lead to more problems than there were to begin with.

Building the Soil You've Got

I'll admit that when we started the farm, I fell for the trap of thinking that (1) purchased soil would be better than the weedy, compacted soil we were inheriting and (2) compost would fix everything. Although our (just under) 2 acres were part of what was originally a small truck farm growing apples and watermelons before eventually housing horses and donkeys in the 50 years prior to our buying it, it had fallen into use as a hybrid driveway and junkyard for old vehicles. The once-fertile soil had been compacted into a concretelike surface and grew nothing but bindweed and other invasive weeds. Half of the main field contained hundreds of old tractor implements and car parts driven into the impenetrable soil. (I once even turned up an entire muffler during planting.) Naturally, I was concerned about heavy metals—part of the reason why we started out growing mostly flowers. Soil tests indicated that we were in the clear to grow produce, but still I decided to bring in 45 yards of the highest-quality compost I could afford. It was expensive, and considering we had no tractor at the time, spreading it by hand was a *lot* of work!

As I learned more about our soil and delved deeper into regenerative agriculture, I realized that I had made a mistake. Subsequent soil tests indicated that the thick compost application had caused my phosphorus levels to skyrocket, potentially affecting the uptake of other nutrients, such as zinc and iron. Through trial and error in other new planting areas, I found there was a better (and cheaper!) way to revitalize our soil. We now use a much more affordable method I've termed the native soil method that creates wonderful soil in a relatively short period of time, takes fewer outside resources, and costs significantly less than trucking in yards of compost and soil. Before we dive into this method, here are a few reasons to avoid purchasing and bringing in soil from offsite.

The Case Against Purchasing Soil

Although there may be some situations where using the existing soil isn't possible (soil that is contaminated with heavy metals or other chemicals, for example, or where container growing is necessary due to bedrock soils), the soil you start with is usually significantly better than soil you can buy. Bagged soils have often been steam sterilized and are devoid of soil life. Some soil companies will add microbes back in after the sterilization process, but the bags are then trucked to garden centers where the soil sits in the sun and steams inside the plastic—and high temperatures can kill off any microbial life within the soil. This also leads to the soils being contaminated by micro- and nanoplastics.

Store-bought soil is lighter and fluffier than what is in native soils. And while this can make planting more enjoyable, fluffy does not necessarily a good soil make.

POTENTIAL CONTAMINATION

Labeling requirements for soils are very lax, leading to the possibility of contamination with unwanted components.

PFAS. Not only can purchased soil be inconsistent between batches, but it can also contain concerning ingredients such as biosolids

When we purchased the farm in the winter of 2018, there was an overgrowth of invasive plants (along the left side of the photo), and the ground was compacted and full of automobile parts and weeds.

(also called biosludge, the human waste sewage by-product from wastewater treatment). Biosolids are known to contain high levels of plastics and may be contaminated with chemicals such as PFAS (per- and polyfluoroalkyl substances). These "forever chemicals" can be taken up into your garden plants, thus into your food. In the United States, companies are not required to label soil products as containing biosolids (in fact, labeling for soils in general is quite vague, making it difficult to determine contents). The exception to this is OMRI-certified (Organic Materials Review Institute) soils and composts, which are not allowed to have biosolids as a component.

Plastics. Macro- and microplastics are both found in bagged soils and can be difficult to track. Bagged soils stored and transported in plastic containers and subjected to high temperatures/moisture can experience this plastic contamination. This, along with the inclusion of biosolids and plastic-contaminated composts in bagged soils, can lead to unknowingly filling your garden with microplastics that can work their way into your homegrown produce. Buying an organic-certified soil will help you avoid biosludge but not necessarily microplastics.

Persistent herbicides. These are another major issue when it comes to purchasing soil. Bulk and bagged soils generally contain some compost for added fertility—but what that compost consists of is often a mystery. Composts with horse manure, for example, may contain persistent herbicides that were present in animal

This simple compost pile is made of old pallet wood and is surrounded by leaf towers made of wire that contain leaves.

feed and that can remain active even after passing through the animal. While most bagged composts have been aged long enough to avoid this, buying bulk composts of unknown origin means concerns of persistent herbicides, and it can be next to impossible to find out the exact composition of the bulk soil you purchase without conducting laboratory testing first.

UNNECESSARY EXPENSE

Although buying soil is necessary for those who can only garden in containers, it is an unnecessary expense for those of us with in-ground beds (or space that could become in-ground beds, such as converted lawns). The cost of soil adds up when you have to fill up a tall raised bed, even if you are purchasing cheap soil and using practices such as filling it in with sticks and leaves. Not to mention the back-breaking labor of shoveling all that soil! And while there are some excellent raised-bed soils out there (such as the potting soil we use in our seed-starting recipe on page 85), they are quite costly.

ENVIRONMENTAL COSTS

Purchasing heavy soil packaged in disposable plastic bags and shipped long distances is unsustainable and comes with a high carbon footprint. It can take 10 or more bags to fill a single raised bed. Regenerating the soil we already have is not only easier on our wallets, it also eliminates the environmental impact of shipping soil.

The bottom line is that we don't always know what's in the bags of soil we purchase—and that can lead to poor garden performance for years. Regeneration may require more patience than conventional practices, but even the worst soil can, in time, be made growable. Whether it's sandy, rocky, or clay, with organic matter and the soil food web behind us, we are capable of converting any soil to healthy, productive soil.

Before You Amend Your Soil, Test It

Understanding soil and how to improve it with amendments is central to regenerative gardening. It also can end up saving you quite a bit of money: Ranging from around $45 to $100, a soil test is an investment that will tell you exactly what needs to be added (or, more frequently, what does *not* need to be added) for optimal soil performance. For example, the heavy clay soils of my area are excellent at retaining minerals as well as storing and fixing phosphorus. However, too much phosphorus can prevent plants from utilizing other nutrients, such as iron and zinc. (Remember that time I applied too much compost? Oops!) Therefore, the common recommendation to use phosphorus fertilizer every two weeks to "get more tomatoes" is not only unnecessary for my particular soil, it can create an excess of phosphorus that would be detrimental to the plants and to my pocketbook as well!

Soil testing can be a great tool for understanding soil makeup and health, especially when first making the shift to regenerative gardening. If, for example, a gardener has long relied on fertilizers to achieve good plant yields, getting a soil test can be useful to confirm how the soil has been affected by that practice over the years. Soil tests can also be helpful and encouraging for monitoring your ongoing progress in the garden. The good news is, if you follow regenerative practices, soil testing is largely a short-term necessity, compared to relying on outside amendments and garden inputs to nourish the soil.

GET A BASELINE MEASUREMENT FROM A SOIL LAB

While physical and visual examination, partnered with evaluation of plant performance, will give you a good idea of the health of your soil, laboratory testing can provide additional information. A soil test reveals nutrient levels, how much organic matter is available, soil pH, and whether the soil contains any dangerous contaminants such as lead. Ongoing lab testing isn't strictly necessary if you are following regenerative practices in the garden, but if you are a results-oriented gardener, it can provide a good measurement of your practices over time, as it will show increases in organic matter and let you know whether you are applying excess compost (this will typically show up as an elevated phosphorus level). Retesting soil once every four to five years would suffice.

Conventional soil tests. There are many reliable soil labs that provide soil reports, including those at state university extension services. These basic tests measure pH as well as phosphorus, potassium, calcium, and other minerals. However, these conventional soil tests have limited usefulness from a regenerative gardening standpoint, because most of them are conducted in the same manner that they were 60 years ago—before we knew about the soil microbiome. Although they give nutrient and mineral levels, which are important, they don't necessarily reflect the entire soil health from the perspective of the soil food web. Traditional soil tests rely on strong, (low-pH) acids to extract nutrients from a soil sample, and they don't measure for the nutrients made available in the presence of an active soil food web that can process organic matter into additional plant nutrients.

Since scientists have learned about the rhizosphere and the abundance of soil life needed for healthy gardens, there have been many efforts to modernize soil testing to get more accurate information based on the new data, specifically by looking at indicators of the presence of microbiology and how that affects the nutrients available to plants.

The Haney Test

Dr. Rick Haney developed a modernized soil test methodology to analyze soil's nutrient balance, respiration, and organic matter content using weaker organic acids designed to mimic root exudate chemistry (see page 207 for labs that perform Haney tests). A Haney test will measure the water-soluble organic carbon and nitrogen in the soil, as well as the ratio of carbon to nitrogen: basically, the amount of "food" available to the microbes in the soil that can then be made available for plants. The Haney test also measures the rate of soil respiration, which is the amount of CO_2 released by the soil microbes and plant roots as a by-product of the decomposition of organic matter. The higher the rate of respiration, the healthier the soil food web. The test is conducted by drying the sample thoroughly before rewetting (to simulate a rainfall event, activating microbes) and measuring respiration of the soil along with other numbers.

Haney tests are helping farmers learn that they don't need as many amendments (nitrogen, in particular) as was previously believed, saving them money. This same test can be as helpful for home and small-farm gardens as it can for large-scale producers and is similar in cost to traditional soil testing. After establishing your garden's baseline, you won't need to retest each year, especially if you follow the seasonal plan outlined later in the book (see page 200).

Because the native soils method relies on regenerative practices such as cover cropping, changes in soil health will be slow and steady rather than rapid, so there is no need to test frequently—so, as with other soil tests, it's not a requirement to retest your soil at all (as compared to conventional gardening, in which the frequent use of amendments such as bloom fertilizers can create a buildup of potentially harmful high phosphorus levels in soils, so it's important to test those soils more regularly). If, however, you are interested in tracking the progression of your soil profile from a scientific standpoint, you can get a Haney soil test from a lab every four to five years.

Clear back mulch and dig down below the surface of the soil to obtain samples for a soils test.

INTERPRETING HANEY TEST NUMBERS

While explaining Haney test data could be a book in and of itself, it's worth going over a few important numbers you'll want to look at if you're getting a Haney soil test.

Soil respiration. Measures how much CO_2-C (the amount of carbon dioxide expressed as the mass of carbon it contains) soil produces in 24 hours following a drying/rewetting event (mimicking a rainfall). More CO_2 means more microbial activity and a higher potential for nutrient cycling and organic matter creation. Less than 10 ppm is very low; over 200 ppm is very high. The higher the number, the better.

Water-extractable organic carbon (WEOC). Measures organic carbon, or the food source available to microbes. It tells you the *quality* of the organic matter in your soil. Native and perennial systems are typically higher in organic carbon than annual beds. The range measured is 100 to 300 ppm, and higher the number (the closer to 300 ppm), the better. This number will fluctuate during the season and will be lower in colder seasons. Inputs such as composts and cover cropping can help increase this number.

Water-extractable organic nitrogen (WEON). Measures organic nitrogen available to microbes. It acts like an amino acid, boosting the amount of carbon that microbes consume. The higher the number, the less added nitrogen you will need.

Organic nitrogen release. This is the overall nitrogen credit given to your soil and depends on the carbon-to-nitrogen ratio present in the soil. The higher the respiration, the more microbes present and the greater the potential for activity and mineralization of nitrogen. While conventional farms might have a range of 9.5 to 10.3, my own farm, with its healthy soil, has an organic N release of 40.

Soil health score. This number summarizes soil respiration, WEOC, and WEON numbers and offers a quick assessment of your soil's overall current health status. It ranges from 0 to 50, with few agricultural soils surpassing 30.

Haney Test Results: A Comparison of Three Beds

Two years ago, I decided to create beds using these three methods and do a Haney soil test on each to find out the effects of the preparation methods on soil health. We built three beds in late summer:

- A "no-dig" bed—cardboard with 4 to 6 inches of compost on top
- A "lasagna" bed—carbon-rich "browns" layered with nitrogen-rich green debris, topped with 2 to 3 inches of compost
- A bed utilizing my "native soil method"—a scant ½-inch to 1 inch of compost tilled into the soil, in which a cover crop is grown and terminated prior to planting (see page 59)

We used the same compost in each bed and allowed them all to lie fallow over winter/spring. In late spring, we tested the soil in all three beds.

Note that the lasagna and no-dig methods both utilize large amounts of compost, meaning we had to buy it to build the beds to the recommended depth. Most home gardeners are simply not able to produce enough compost to build garden beds using these methods. We bought the highest-quality compost we could find in our area: OMRI certified, free of biosolids, and well aged.

CO_2 Respiration

Carbon dioxide respiration is an indicator of the soil's ability to "breathe" and therefore is also an indicator of its level of microbial activity.

The no-dig bed. Even though this method is touted to minimally affect the soil microbial life, it resulted in the lowest respiration level. This is in line with the hypothesis that cardboard forms an oxygen- and moisture-impermeable barrier when placed on top of the soil, effectively smothering existing soil life underneath, especially when topped with an additional 4 to 6 inches of compost.

Although we might think that the compost would have high levels of microbial activity, this varies widely from one batch of compost to another, and it depends on how long the compost has been sitting and how it has been stored. It's likely that the soil life will eventually recover and colonize into the compost after the cardboard breaks down, but it will take at least a season. Adding mycorrhizae and compost teas will help resuscitate it more quickly.

The lasagna bed. This had higher levels of CO_2 respiration than the no-dig method, likely because of the addition of microbial life in the green layers of leaves, oats, and grass added throughout the layers of the lasagna.

The native soil bed. The winner for microbial respiration was the native soil method. This illustrates that tillage—which aerates the soil—is not necessarily the worst way to first establish a garden bed and remove existing plant roots, when compared to no-dig and lasagna smothering methods.

Levels of Organic Matter and Nitrogen Release

The beds that used large quantities of compost had higher levels of organic matter and organic nitrogen release—that is, nitrogen available for microbe mineralization—than the native soil method. However, they also had extremely high levels of phosphorus and soluble salt levels, likely due to the presence of animal manure, making the compost a poor choice to use as a growing medium, especially in the first year (though the effects would decrease over time with thorough watering and aging). High phosphorus levels can result in leaching into nearby waterways, leading to the death of aquatic life, and can also affect nutrient uptake by plants.

Haney Test Results

The table below shows the test results that we found surprising and relevant to garden health. The results for these methods indicate that compost is most effective when used cautiously as an amendment, rather than as a growing medium. It also indicates that, although repeated tilling can harm soil health over time, an *initial* tilling to establish a bed can be helpful in improving soil respiration.

	No-Dig Method	Lasagna Method	Native Soil Method
CO_2 respiration	120.2	251.0	270.9
Organic matter	11.3%	13.5%	8.2%
Soluble salts	3.74	5.34	0.86
Organic nitrogen release	58.5	94.1	50.1
Phosphorus	568	651	232

Testing for Heavy Metals

Of course, there is one more consideration to make when starting a planting bed, and that is whether your existing soil is safe for growing in. In areas around older homes, which may have been painted with lead paint, or places where cars may have sat and left residues from motor oils and gasoline that can leach into the soil, it may not be safe to grow food for consumption.

Conducting a heavy metals contamination test (available from soil testing labs) is recommended before making plans for beds if you aren't sure of the history of your property and growing area. It can be dangerous to consume food grown in soil with metals such as lead, barium, nickel, chromium, mercury, cadmium, and arsenic, so testing is best when in doubt. If soils are contaminated, grow ornamentals instead of edible plants in that area, or consider using phytoremediation plants such as cover crops (sunflowers are an excellent phytoremediator, as are hemp and many grassy cover crops like Sudan grass). Phytoremediators extract a wide range of heavy metals and organic pollutants from the soil and can be helpful in situations where heavy metals exist. Retest the soil after a couple of years to verify the success of these plants, or consider siting your garden in a different location.

There are places on our farm where we know machinery and farm equipment maintenance took place or where contaminants build up (such as alongside the driveway), and we grow sunflowers to help remove those. I typically dispose of the resulting sunflower biomass in the landfill at the end of the season rather than compost it, since phytoremediators such as sunflowers take the contaminants up into the plant itself. Research on phytoremediators is still evolving, but at this time I advise against using the waste from plants grown in contaminated soils in your compost system until further studies indicate this is safe.

After Your Soil Tests

A Haney soil test can provide good baseline information such as levels of soil respiration, organic matter content, soil texture, mineral deficiencies, and nutrient levels, but the annual soil management practices I outline in the regenerative seasonal guide (page 200) will be the same regardless. The only thing a soil test might change is the amount of compost you use or the types of cover crops you choose to implement in the garden.

This is the most paradigm-shifting and rewarding part of regenerative gardening. Once you have these strategies and practices down, you can apply them no matter the type of soil or region you are growing in. While a soil test can be helpful at the beginning of the journey, we are able to ascertain a lot about the soil quality by the performance of the plants themselves.

We planted sunflowers on either side of the old driveway at the farm to help remove residual heavy metals from the soil.

How to Take Samples for Soil Testing

Use the following guide to collect soil samples for all testing, whether using Haney or conventional soil testing.

Dig the correct depth. Take samples from 2 to 6 inches below the surface, using a rust-free spade (rust can throw off mineral levels in samples). Take all the samples at the same depth. Gather about ½ cup of soil per sample. Take approximately five samples per growing space.

Combine samples. Thoroughly combine the sample soils in a clean bucket or mixing bowl to create a homogenous mixture. Place 2 cups of the mixture into a bag clearly labeled with your name, address, and phone number. If you are testing several growing areas with different soil types, consider submitting more than one sample for evaluation.

Ship it off. *Immediately* send the sample to the lab for best results. If you cannot send it immediately, store the bag in the fridge for up to two weeks; but the sooner, the better.

Keep it regular. Unless you add a lot of amendments to your soil, it isn't necessary to test yearly (unless you want to), but if you want to track changes in your soil, test every three to five years. Do it at the same time each year to properly track trends.

For each sample, take soil from multiple spots and mix it together to get an idea of average data. If your garden locations are very spread apart or there are multiple beds, sending in a few samples is best, one for each.

Starting Garden Beds: An Overview of Options

There is so much information available about starting garden beds that it can be overwhelming and confusing to try to figure out the best method for your soil's health. Many of us are working with existing lawns, rocky soil, or other challenging landscapes rather than starting with a blank canvas. In this section, we'll explore some of the most popular methods for creating garden beds and weigh their pros and cons.

None of the strategies I outline here is right or wrong; some are simply more suited to specific conditions and situations. The key to success—and saving money!—is "know thy soil." By assessing soil structure, existing weeds, and the materials and tools that are readily available, you can make more informed decisions. Knowing all of these strategies, along with their benefits and drawbacks, will help you find the best approach for your situation.

It is more environmentally sound and most economical to grow in existing native soil, if at all possible. While raised beds are popular due to their ease of assembly, they are also costly and require lots of purchased soil, which can be contaminated or imbalanced. If growing in a raised bed or container is your only option (for instance, if your soil is contaminated with heavy metals, you are limited to gardening on a balcony or patio, or you have mobility issues), we will discuss economical and environmentally friendly ways to fill them (see page 70).

The process of building a garden bed is twofold. The first step is to remove existing vegetation that may compete with desired plants, and the second is to improve the soil and create a functioning soil food web within the space. Let's look at some common methods for starting beds and how they fit with the idea of gardening regeneratively.

This new garden bed was established by removing existing vegetation and followed by cover cropping to help provide beneficial organic matter and bolster the soil food web.

A no-dig bed is layered with cardboard to smother existing vegetation, followed by a layer of compost. This method may also smother existing soil life.

A lasagna method garden bed immediately after building. These beds are most successful when left to sit several months before planting.

Starting Garden Beds by Layering on Top of Vegetation

You can start a garden bed simply by layering materials over the top of existing vegetation.

THE NO-DIG METHOD

This is one of the most popular methods for growing in the ground, and it uses simple and accessible techniques. The no-dig method calls for a layer of cardboard to be placed on top of existing weeds or lawn, followed by 6 to 8 inches of compost, which then can be planted into immediately. The benefit of this method is that it is easy to quickly smother any existing vegetation.

The downside, of course, is that it requires a great deal of compost—more than most of us are able to produce on a home garden scale. This means that the no-dig method typically requires us to turn to bagged or bulk composts. And while there are good ones out there, it is difficult to know the contents of our compost or the nutrient makeup. (See What's Wrong with Purchased Compost? on page 56.) A potential downside of using cardboard is the lack of information about its exact material makeup. Recycled cardboards can contain any number of inputs, possibly including contaminants such as PFAS, or "forever chemicals." Cardboard has also been shown to smother soil life via oxygen deprivation, which is counterintuitive to the idea of this garden method being better for the soil food web.

THE LASAGNA METHOD

Lasagna gardening begins much the same way as the no-dig method but relies less on purchased compost and more on additional organic matter in the form of garden scraps, leaves, grass, paper, etc. A base layer of cardboard is applied to smother the existing weeds and vegetation, and on top is placed alternating layers of greens (wet, recently growing plant material) and browns (dry or woody plant material), topped with 2 to 4 inches of topsoil or compost.

The hügelkultur method is quite similar, though typically it uses large logs and branches at the bottom of the pile and results in a taller mound.

While the lasagna method is slightly less risky than the no-dig method because it uses less compost of unknown origins, it still requires a large quantity of grass clippings, straw, and other materials. Shredded paper is also frequently recommended as a layer within the lasagna garden. Again, be aware of the materials' sources: Were any of them treated with herbicides that will remain in the soil and contaminate the garden? Care must be taken when sourcing materials for the lasagna garden.

As is true of the no-dig method, concerns remain about the contents of cardboard and even shredded paper. Do they contain residual PFAS, which is notoriously common in paper products?

Both the lasagna and no-dig methods are done in the name of not disturbing the soil life through tillage. We now know, however, that soil life is smothered by solid sheets of cardboard (which lack the oxygen and water permeability soil life needs), and the bed is then topped with disturbed and turned soil, so extra steps will be needed to regrow and support soil life with these methods.

Starting Garden Beds by Removing Vegetation

There are several methods for removing vegetation from garden beds before you plant.

OCCULTATION

Occultation can be an excellent way to kill existing vegetation and prepare the ground for productive garden space. It consists of wetting the ground to create humidity, followed by covering the area with a clear or black plastic to create and contain heat. The plastic is weighted down and left in place for a minimum of six to eight weeks during the hottest months of summer to create enough heat to kill the grasses to a depth of several inches. It will also sterilize any existing weed seeds on the surface, minimizing the weeds that will germinate once the plastic is removed.

The downsides of occultation are that it takes time to be effective, requires a large amount of plastic, doesn't work as well in locations with partial shade, and doesn't kill any deep rhizome-based weeds (such as bindweed) because the soil will not heat to the depth of their roots. The high temperatures that occur at the soil level with occultation also kill many of the fungi and microbes essential to the healthy garden; however, they can be regrown and coaxed back to the soil over time with the addition of compost teas, living plant roots, and quality homemade compost.

I'm preparing to use the occultation method by covering the ground with a black tarp to kill vegetation before planting a garden bed. A clear tarp will also work for this purpose.

TILLING

Tilling, which entails breaking up the soil before planting, can be particularly destructive to soil life, which is why it is generally avoided in the regenerative agriculture space. Over time, it also leads to compacted soil, which is more susceptible to drought and overly wet conditions during times of dryness or of excessive rainfall. Compacted soil also lacks the aeration required for microbial life to thrive.

Repeated tilling and overworking of the soil in general leads to a loss of fungal and microbial life; hence, if you must till to start a garden, know that the soil life will need replenishment and that tilling should be done no more than once every 5 to 10 years. Tilling can also spread weed seeds throughout the garden and lead to the worsening of rhizome-based weeds like bindweed, since new plants sprout from the chopped pieces and the weeds thus multiply in the garden.

SOD REMOVAL

Using a sod cutter or a shovel to remove the top level of sod is a viable means of starting a garden; however, it requires a good deal of manual labor, removes much of the organic matter in the garden, and often doesn't cut deep enough to fully remove many turf grasses and weeds. The biggest advantage is that it can be done quickly.

What's Wrong with Purchased Compost?

Compost is generally a valuable addition to gardens, and it certainly helps the planet when we compost our food and garden remnants rather than put them in the landfill. To use compost properly, it's crucial to understand your existing nutrient levels and tailor compost application accordingly while also using alternative sources of organic matter, such as cover crops.

When store-bought compost is used as the main growing medium or as a major component of soil, it can create problems including phosphorus buildup, especially in gardens with already-elevated phosphorus levels, and can lead to contamination with microplastics, herbicides, and PFAS.

Concerns with Manure

Manure-based composts can introduce additional imbalances or contamination to your soil.

Phosphorus. Many bagged composts contain high levels of manure, which can lead to excess phosphorus buildup in gardens (especially if your soil, like mine, contains clay, is alkaline, and already tends to run high in phosphorus). According to studies conducted by the International Plant Nutrition Institute, gardeners in the United States are applying phosphorus at rates 30 times greater than that applied in US conventional agriculture—so we are really overusing it at home. Reducing the amount of manure applied can help bring this back into balance.

Phosphorus is highly immobile in soil—that is, it tends to stick around, and it creates a buildup that can leach into nearby waterways, leading to eutrophication and the death of aquatic life (the algae blooms in the "dead zone" of the Gulf of Mexico are an example of this). While phosphorus is of concern particularly with manure-based compost, it is a consideration with any compost, all of which contain some level of phosphorus. Over time, this phosphorus builds up in the soil and can lead to deficiencies of other minerals, such as iron, in plants.

Salinity. Manure-based composts can be high in soluble salts, which can impede plants' uptake of nutrient molecules and severely limit vegetative growth. High levels of soluble salts can also lead to an increase in diseases that contribute to root rot, like phytophthora and pythium.

Persistent herbicides. Manure can be contaminated with residual herbicide from animals that grazed on herbicide-treated feed, such as hay that has been treated with persistent herbicides common in agriculture. These herbicides will pass through the digestive system of animals that feed on contaminated crops and can stay active for up to four years, according to Oregon State University research. When added to garden soil, these persistent herbicides can harm and kill plants.

PFAS Contamination

Another concern with compost is the presence of biosolids, or recycled human waste. Municipal waste treatment facilities sell or give this to composting facilities (which are not required to disclose the contents of their compost). Recycling human waste into compost is problematic because of the heavy metals and PFAS it contains.

Studies have shown that PFAS are carcinogens and endocrine disruptors. They have also shown that plants grown in contaminated soil take up PFAS, which leads to contamination of the food that is produced. This has already happened on a large scale in Maine. In the 1980s and 1990s, more than 75 percent of Maine's biosolids were recycled into topsoil and compost products that were made available to homeowners and farms. Testing in 2016 indicated extremely high levels of PFAS contamination in several farms that used biosolids as fertilizer or in compost applications; this led Maine to ban the use of biosolids in 2022.

Unfortunately, other states are failing to create such laws, continuing the trade and sale of

biosolids to homeowners and farms. There is no regulation requiring that compost components, including biosolids, be listed on packaging. As you might guess, it is incredibly difficult to know what is in your compost if you aren't making it yourself.

Guidelines for Using Purchased Compost

Sourcing compost from reputable and certified suppliers who ensure quality control and screen for contaminants is essential. By using compost judiciously and responsibly, gardeners can harness its potential benefits for enriching soil while minimizing phosphorus excess, microplastics, herbicides, and PFAS.

Here are a few tips to help you source and use compost in a way that won't create problems.

Ask what's in it and how old it is. Make sure your supplier can tell you exactly what is in the compost and how long it has been aging. They should be able to provide you with up-to-date soil tests that have been done on their compost.

Verify that biosolids (a.k.a. biosludge or human waste) have not been used. If you want to be sure there are no biosolids, look for the OMRI certification seal on bagged compost. While any bag of soil can be labeled "organic," the OMRI certification ensures that the bag will not contain biosolids.

Don't overapply. One inch per year is plenty. Recipes for garden soil that require 4 or more inches of compost can lead to issues, so remember—less is more!

When in doubt, age the compost in place. Get it delivered in fall and let it sit for the winter; the longer it ages, the less you will need to be concerned with salinity and herbicide contamination, as those levels lessen over time. This will not work for PFAS or plastic-contaminated compost, however, so again: Verify the components of the compost!

Test it. Fill a small pot with the purchased compost and start a radish or bean seed. If the seed germinates and quickly becomes yellow, the compost isn't ready for use and needs additional aging.

Examine the compost when it is delivered or purchased. If you find plastic pieces or trash, refuse the shipment or return the bag for a refund, and don't purchase that brand again.

Low-Input Regenerative Garden Beds

Establishing new garden beds with a regenerative approach involves mindful practices that prioritize soil health, avoiding contaminants, and sustainability. These methods take longer than the quick methods above, but they are more supportive of soil life and promote a healthier, more sustainable foundation for future garden spaces. The three regenerative methods outlined here are organized by how long they take to establish.

Fastest: Leaf layering. This is the quickest method and involves scalping existing vegetation, putting down a layer of leaves, and topping with planting soil. It is more costly because it requires additional inputs in the form of soil and compost. While it is the most expensive (unless you have free access to good planting soil), this method will result in an immediately plantable garden bed.

Fast/Moderate: The native soil method. Also known as tilling and cover cropping, the native soil method focuses on removing existing grass through tilling and then nurturing the soil life back to health via a cover crop. Although the cover crop can be omitted for immediate planting, the cover crop will help heal the soil and will take 8 to 10 weeks to grow, terminate, and be ready for planting into.

Slow: The deep-mulch method. If you have time and patience, this method involves spreading deep layers of organic mulch to create plantable, nutrient-rich soil without tilling. It takes approximately a year, but the results are worth it.

Bear in mind that the slower the method, the more beneficial and less detrimental it will be for soil life. Which one you use will depend on what materials you have access to and how much time and patience you have. You can also mix and match the following methods. Remember, these are merely a loose guide.

Note that each of the three following methods assume that you are starting these beds on an existing lawn or compacted soil that doesn't contain invasive rhizome-based weeds such as bindweed or Bermuda grass. See page 64 for information on dealing with spaces containing rhizomatous weeds.

The deep-mulch method contributes to a nutrient-rich soil environment.

Fastest: Leaf Layering

The regenerative methods prescribed in this book are not quick fixes. It takes time and patience to achieve balanced soil with these methods. That said, sometimes we need to establish garden beds more quickly. The leaf-layering method is the fastest of the regenerative approaches, and it allows you to plant into the beds immediately. This method assumes the gardener has access to organic matter such as leaves or dried herbicide-free grass clippings to form a suppressive layer, as well as to homemade or OMRI-certified bagged garden soils and composts.

Cut back existing vegetation. Begin by cutting back vegetation as close as you can to ground level. Removing the competing plants while leaving their roots intact facilitates a quick decomposition process.

Mulch with leaves or grass clippings. Next, create a barrier by applying a 3- to 4-inch layer of finely shredded leaves or grass clippings (untreated by herbicides) over the exposed soil, and water the mulch so that it settles. (This is instead of using cardboard, as in the no-dig and lasagna methods. The shredded leaves allow oxygen and water to percolate through to the soil. They also don't contain the toxic compounds potentially found in cardboard.) Not only does the leaf mulch help suppress regrowth, but it also introduces organic matter that enriches the soil as it quickly decomposes.

Top with soil. On top of the leaves, add a 4- to 6-inch layer of OMRI-certified garden soil (or soil from your property, if possible—for example, soil left over from excavating for garden pathways), which will hold the leaves down and add nutrients without risk of contamination with synthetic chemicals and biosolids. Add in an additional 2 inches of OMRI-certified compost if using dirt from your property that appears low in organic matter. Incorporating this nutrient-rich soil into the prepared bed provides an optimal environment for new plants, fostering rapid growth and establishing a healthy foundation for your garden.

When it comes time to plant, seedlings will go into this top layer of soil. If you build the bed in the fall, it will have settled by springtime—partially because the leaves will have begun to decompose (and may or may not be visible when you plant).

Add alfalfa fertilizer and plant. Mix a couple of tablespoons of alfalfa fertilizer (see page 190) into the dirt in the planting hole before planting seedlings. Water the plant and surrounding soil thoroughly. Top with an additional layer of organic mulch (see page 96 for mulch suggestions).

Fast to Moderate: The Native Soil Method

This method is one I've termed "the native soil method" because it uses the existing soil on-site, along with a scant amount of homemade compost (if possible) to avoid creating imbalances in the soil. It employs a surface-level till to remove existing plant roots, make the soil more workable, and mix in a small amount of compost for organic matter. It also provides a good seedbed for starting a cover crop, which prevents erosion and adds organic matter to the soil as it decomposes. By cultivating a diverse cover crop mix, gardeners can naturally enhance soil fertility and structure without relying heavily on external amendments. Using inoculated seed and regular applications of compost tea (see page 186) will help soil microbes and fungi recover after tillage.

The downside is that this takes advance planning if you intend to plant a cover crop. We begin in late summer to be ready for garden planting the next spring, but it can also be done in early spring for a late-summer planting. If you're starting in late spring, use an early-germinating, cold-tolerant cover crop such as peas; terminate (kill) them in midsummer; and plant cool-season crops such as beets, lettuce, and kale for a fall harvest.

If time is short, you can still use this method—just skip the cover crop. Use the compost tea and alfalfa fertilizer recipes from pages 186 and 190 to help soil recover from the disturbance.

LEAF LAYERING STEP BY STEP

1. Mow down existing vegetation using a lawnmower at its lowest setting.
2. Layer leaves and (optional) dried grass clippings at a depth of 3 to 4 inches.
3. Top with soil and compost from your site or with OMRI-certified garden soil. Do not use potting soil.
4. Plant into the soil, adding a couple of tablespoons of alfalfa fertilizer to each hole. Top-dress around plants with the mulch of your choice.

THE NATIVE SOIL METHOD STEP BY STEP

This method not only accelerates garden-bed preparation but also ensures a sustainable, low-input, and nutrient-rich foundation for your plants.

1. **Withhold moisture.** Stop watering the area to weaken the existing plants and grass. Use occultation for more pernicious weeds (see page 55).
2. **Till to loosen.** Repeated tillage is bad for soil life, but an initial till to loosen the existing soil can be helpful, particularly if there is still live grass to be removed or if the soil is heavily compacted.
3. **Remove plants.** Collect clumps of vegetation by hand and compost them, as long as no invasive weeds are present. Discard any vegetation containing invasive weeds or plant matter that has been treated with herbicides.
4. **Water and wait.** Irrigate the area and wait two weeks for regrowth.
5. **Repeat till.** Till again to create a finer, more workable soil texture, and remove vegetation (or solarize if the area was very weedy). Incorporate 1 to 2 inches of OMRI-certified compost or homemade compost during the final tillage to provide an immediate boost of nutrients to the soil.
6. **Plant a cover crop.** Follow with a cover crop according to your soil type and goals (see page 158); inoculate the cover crop (see page 184) by rubbing a small amount of moist homemade compost onto seeds prior to planting. Drench soil with compost tea weekly until frost.
7. **Terminate the cover crop.** Do this at or just before the flowering stage and before seed set. Wait two weeks before planting. (See page 149.)
8. **Plant.** When you are ready, simply move the cover crop residue aside and plant. The cover crop material serves as mulch and protects the soil, retains moisture, and promotes a good environment for the soil food web to thrive. Add a couple of tablespoons of the alfalfa fertilizer (see page 190) to each planting hole if a legume-based cover crop was not used in step 6.

Tilling loosens the existing native soil to make vegetation removal easier.

Remove clumps of grass after they've been loosened from tillage.

Cover crops emerge from the tilled area. These can be planted before or after the last frost if cold-tolerant crops are selected.

To terminate a buckwheat cover crop by hand, crimp it to break the stems.

Slow: The Deep-Mulch Method

For those with a bit more patience, my favorite method for starting new beds is applying deep layers (at least 8 inches) of organic mulch to create plantable spaces without tilling. This method involves covering the designated area with materials like leaves and thick layers of wood chips, allowing the existing vegetation to decompose beneath. As the deep mulch breaks down, it not only suppresses weeds but also contributes to a nutrient-rich soil environment. While this creates microbially healthy planting soil, it also takes the longest (a year at minimum, though the mulch can be left in place for an extended time until you are ready to plant).

When we first moved to our farm, we unintentionally started several planting beds this way. In the rear of the property, there was a massive pile of wood chips from trees that had been cleared. One of the first things I did was spread the pile in the back corner of the property, just to get it out of the way. It was the same spot where we had a thicket of invasive thistles growing every year, but the soil was too heavy and compacted for us to pull them. The next year, we went to build our new compost pile where I had spread the chips, and I was shocked at the change in the soil composition. Where we pulled the decomposed chips away, the soil was full of life, crumbly, rich, and moist: a stark difference from the dry, cracked, compacted area we started with. What few thistles were still growing through the thick mulch came easily out of the soil—such a satisfying feeling!

Covering the soil with mulch rather than cardboard or plastic allows moisture to reach the soil surface and the soil to respire. Instead of killing the soil life, the mulching method encourages it to proliferate, thanks to an abundance of organic matter, air, and water.

THE DEEP-MULCH METHOD STEP BY STEP

1. **Cut back plants.** Cut the existing vegetation all the way down to soil level using a lawnmower at its lowest setting.
2. **Cover and wait.** Completely cover the future bed with at least 8 inches of wood chips. Let it sit undisturbed for at least a year.
3. **Move and plant.** After a year has passed, simply move the mulch aside and plant directly into the rich soil—you can rake the mulch off into a wheelbarrow and reuse it elsewhere if you are seeding the bed, or just scooch it aside if you are planting plugs or seedlings. Keep the area watered to assist with breakdown.
4. **Repeat.** Use the same mulch to smother a new area if it is still intact.

A note on mulches: When selecting wood chips for deep mulching in the garden, avoid any that may have adverse effects on soil health.

Adding wood chips to the soil provides many benefits that foster a thriving soil food web:

- As wood chips gradually decompose, they release organic matter, providing a continuous source of carbon that feeds and energizes a diverse array of microorganisms. This influx of carbon supports the growth and activity of beneficial bacteria and fungi, crucial players in cycling the nutrients that are then made available to plants.
- The wood chips provide shelter and moisture retention, creating an environment conducive to soil-dwelling organisms, such as earthworms, beetles, and other decomposers.
- The slow breakdown of wood chips enhances soil structure, promoting aeration and water infiltration.

In essence, the incorporation of wood chips into the soil acts as a catalyst for a flourishing soil food web, contributing to a healthier, more dynamic ecosystem that nurtures plant growth and overall soil vitality.

Another benefit of this method is that it allows you to convert larger areas to productive garden space a little bit at a time. Preparing the beds in advance cuts down on doing everything at once, which can be both overwhelming and prohibitively expensive. You might establish one area using a different method in one season while using the deep-mulch method in the meantime on another area to be planted the following season. For example, I used the deep-mulch method when we converted large areas of Kentucky bluegrass to native grasses and plants. Doing the whole space at once would have been overwhelming, but by adopting the deep-mulch method, we could prepare one section at a time and focus on other projects while the mulch broke down. Once we were ready to plant the new areas, they were all prepped and ready to go. The downside to this method, of course, is that it doesn't provide instant gratification!

- Steer clear of bagged, dyed mulches, which can contain recycled wood from unknown sources and could potentially be chemically treated.
- Avoid using only black walnut tree chips, which contain juglone, a growth restrictor in plants.
- Avoid chips from diseased or infested trees to prevent the spread of pests such as the ash borer or diseases like thousand canker.

To acquire large amounts of safe and beneficial wood chips, consider reaching out to local arborists or tree removal services, and sign up for free wood chips at chipdrop.com. Many arborists are willing to provide wood chips for free, as it saves them disposal costs (though we find a tip helps and is appreciated!). Municipal tree services and recycling centers are other potential sources. Community-based programs, like those promoting responsible Christmas tree disposal and mulching initiatives, can also provide wood chips.

A year after layering the bed with the deep-mulch method, a rich, loamy soil is left behind.

What If I Have Pernicious Invasive or Rhizome-Based Weeds?

If you are dealing with invasive weeds such as bindweed and Bermuda grass, starting a garden bed without causing any soil damage poses a nuanced challenge. Each approach has pros and cons, but whatever method you use, it is vital that these plants be fully removed before you start your garden bed—otherwise, the result will be failure, frustration, and money down the drain. Ultimately, the choice depends on your priorities, your environmental values, and the unique characteristics of the weed species. With a thoughtful and informed decision-making process, you can remove the weeds and establish a garden bed without causing undue harm to the soil.

Manual removal. This involves physically uprooting the invasive weeds, which preserves the soil structure but demands significant time and effort. Hand-pulling or digging out weeds is effective for smaller infestations. Be sure to remove the entire root system to prevent regrowth. Manual removal is not as effective for most deep-rooted rhizome weeds such as bindweed, which can regrow from tiny pieces of remaining root and often go very deep into the soil profile.

Occultation. This uses sunlight to control weeds by trapping heat beneath a plastic cover. The main advantage is its simplicity: It requires minimal effort and no chemical inputs. The process effectively eliminates many weed seeds, pathogens, and pests, promoting a clean slate for planting. However, there are notable drawbacks. Occultation demands consistent sunlight and high temperatures, making it less effective in cooler climates or during cloudy periods. Additionally, the technique can disrupt the balance of beneficial soil organisms, impacting the overall soil ecosystem. The plastic used in occultation raises environmental concerns like microplastic contamination in the soil. Occultation can take a long time to be successful. It also may not eliminate weeds, such as bindweed, which has very deep taproots extending many feet below soil level.

Herbicides. This is a quicker solution but risks harming both beneficial soil life and human health. Though using organic-certified or horticultural vinegar–based herbicides has been generally accepted as a more environmentally friendly option than synthetic chemicals, these can still cause harm and kill soil life. Be cautious with concentrations to avoid harm to soil organisms. Vinegar may be effective on some weeds but will not be effective on rhizome-based plants because it only kills aboveground foliage. In some cases, as with invasive weeds like Japanese knotweed, cautiously painting herbicide with a brush onto the plants after cutting may be the sole option, and it requires only a one-time treatment if done at the right time and with the proper herbicide. Consult your state extension service for recommendations on when and how to use these, or hire a certified applicator.

Boiling water. Pouring boiling water directly on weeds can be an effective, chemical-free method. This is especially useful for weeds growing in pavement cracks or along borders, but it likely won't kill belowground growth.

Competition planting. Introduce other plants to overshadow and outcompete the invaders. This promotes biodiversity and requires strategic planning. Introducing competitive plants that naturally suppress weeds can help control invasive species without harming the soil. Select ground covers or dense plantings to outcompete weeds for sunlight and nutrients. We've found native grasses like big bluestem and switchgrass are highly effective at outcompeting rhizome-based weeds such as bindweed due to their deep taproots, but mechanical control is still required until these plants are established.

Biological control. Introduce or encourage natural predators of specific weeds, such as insects or animals that feed on them. Biological controls like natural predators can be environmentally friendly, yet their effectiveness may vary—bindweed mites, for example, can be effective only on irrigated areas of lawn and garden and take many years to have an impact. This method requires careful consideration to avoid unintended consequences, such as introducing nonnative pieces of the ecosystem (see Store-Bought "Beneficial" Insects, page 71).

Remember, it's essential to choose methods that align with the specific characteristics of the invasive weed and the surrounding ecosystem to minimize impact on beneficial soil life.

Bindweed climbs the fences and covers the ground around a planting of corn at the farm. This area has since been planted densely with native grasses to outcompete the bindweed effectively.

3 Minimize the "Purchased Garden"

TOO OFTEN, we are taught to rely on purchasing bottled and bagged solutions to "fix" perceived problems in the garden. These solutions can include pesticides, fertilizers, bagged soils and composts (which, as we've discussed, can contain a variety of unknown ingredients, nutrient levels, salinity levels, and more), "miracle" products, and even beneficial insects. These are usually expensive and unnecessary and can even result in damage to soil ecology if overapplied. If done correctly, regenerative gardening means you won't apply any artificial fertilizers, chemicals, or other inputs at all, but rather will build up overall garden resiliency by supporting the garden ecosystem and strengthening the soil food web.

Store-Bought Garden Products

My first year of farming was, in a word, *expensive*. The 45 yards of compost, the landscape fabric (yikes, what a mistake that was!), the seeds, tubers, plants, and seed-starting equipment—it all added up, and that was before the growing season even started. The recommendation for fertilizing, according to my bottle of fish emulsion, was to apply weekly. For a garden the size of mine, this would have cost around $200 a month. My decision to stop using fertilizer was initially a cost-saving measure, but it became impossible to ignore the ecological benefits of feeding the soil with cover crops rather than with fertilizers. Five years later, my garden is just as productive using cover crops and soil microbes as the main sources of nutrients as it was using fish emulsion, and it is far less expensive.

Commercial Fertilizers

If you've ever browsed the fertilizer aisle at the garden store, you know that understanding the many options can be overwhelming, and the labels are not necessarily helpful. Different brands of fertilizers contain varying amounts of nitrogen (N), phosphorus (P), and potassium (K), and while the N-P-K numbers on the label indicate how much is present in each bottle, most gardeners have no idea what their soil needs, or whether they need fertilizer at all, and the bottle often recommends using too much.

Bloom fertilizers in particular (even organic ones) contain high levels of phosphorus, which can build up in soil over time. It is also possible to over-fertilize with nitrogen fertilizers such as fish emulsion, which can lead to slow growth and yellowing of plants. These weakened plants can then attract aphids. Excess nitrogen and phosphorus from over-applied fertilizers will often leach into groundwater supplies, rivers, and streams and eventually end up in lakes and oceans, leading to eutrophication, the death of aquatic life, toxic algae, and other serious environmental problems. The Gulf of Mexico dead zone is a sad and telling example of this issue on the macro scale.

Fertilizer runoff is not only an agricultural matter—home gardens are a major contributor. In fact, studies indicate that 20 to 40 times more nutrients are applied to gardens each year than are harvested as produce, so we're using far more than we need. A study conducted in Minnesota's Twin Cities found that although urban gardens make up only 0.1 percent of land area in the Twin Cities, compost application to these urban gardens constitutes one of the largest inputs of phosphorus to the watershed.

Our home gardens may be small, but they make significant contributions to ecosystems—so the choices we make there matter.

This garden bed is brimming with edible and flowering crops. The biodiversity attracts beneficial insects and reduces disease spread despite the tight spacing.

Home gardens are part of broader ecosystems, and the inputs we add to them don't stay in one place. This stream runs through a ditch on our farm and could easily be contaminated with fertilizer runoff, carrying it to a nearby lake.

Bagged Soils and Composts

It is not always possible to avoid purchasing bagged soils (especially when you're container gardening or restricted to balcony growing). But purchasing bags of soil and compost that have been shipped across the country is not only costly, but it also comes with significant ecological impacts. Labeling requirements of bagged soils and composts are minimal, so they can contain many unknown ingredients (such as biosolids). Additionally, in my experience, even high-quality bagged soils can be inconsistent in quality. Due to the nature of shipping, temperature fluctuations, and time spent sitting in bags, they are likely not as rich in microbial life as our existing soils. A local soil provider who can deliver in bulk is a good option, but if purchasing a bagged soil or compost is the only option, try to source OMRI certified.

What to Look for When Purchasing Compost or Soils (Or: Why Source OMRI Certified?)

Does the soil/compost have an OMRI certification? Soils and composts cannot be certified organic by the same organization that certifies produce, but the Organic Materials Review Institute (OMRI) is an independent organization that will certify that soils or composts are approved for organic certification. To receive OMRI certification, composts must be tested regularly to ensure they don't contain persistent herbicides or petrochemical residues. They also cannot contain biosolids. Without this certification, it can be very difficult for gardeners to know what is in bagged soils and composts.

What are the ingredients of the soil/compost? I look for bags that are specific about their contents. If a bag simply says "compost," that's not enough information for me to comfortably ascertain whether it will be high in certain nutrients and buy it. For example, I know that a compost that contains animal manures will likely contain moderate to high levels of phosphorus. OMRI-certified composts must always use organic manure when possible; if not possible, there are regulations for what type can be used, and the source of manure must always be recorded.

Have any of the compost components been contaminated with systemic herbicides? I typically don't worry much about this one if I source OMRI certified, since systemic herbicide–contaminated inputs are not allowed as components of those composts. It can be difficult to know whether "aged manure" products contain systemic herbicides.

Is it made with biosolids (human waste), which can contain PFAs (forever chemicals)? There are no labeling requirements for composts or soils that contain biosolids, so the best way to ensure your soil doesn't contain any is to purchase OMRI-certified soils or composts.

Store-Bought "Beneficial" Insects

The use of beneficial insects has exploded in popularity as the plight of pollinators—whose numbers are dwindling with the effects of changing weather, habitat threats, and the overuse of pesticides—has led gardeners to seek environmentally friendly alternatives to pest control. Purchasing beneficial insects may seem like an innocuous way to support the garden ecosystem and take care of pests such as aphids (after all, ladybugs gobble up thousands of aphids and don't require any kind of chemical application!), but there can be many unintended side effects.

Ladybugs. Ladybugs purchased and released into gardens don't immediately become part of the garden ecosystem. If food and nectar sources aren't already present to sustain the ladybugs, they will simply fly away. If they do stick around, they can skew the delicate balance of the ecosystem or spread disease to the native ladybugs in your area.

Store-bought beneficial insects come *from* somewhere. Ladybugs are often harvested from their natural habitat (in North America, this is mostly in the Sierra Nevada and in Colorado) during their hibernation phase. The damage done by removing billions of these creatures from their native habitat has not been fully studied, but it is expected to have a significant impact to their home ecosystem.

The goal, instead, is to let the ecosystem equalize naturally on its own while supporting it through the installation of native plants evolved to attract their pollinator populations. While the best plants to use for this goal will depend on your specific ecoregion, ladybugs in general prefer umbel-shaped flowers such as golden alexanders (*Zizia aurea* and *Z. aptera*).

Praying Mantids. Praying mantids can be great allies in the garden and are voracious predators that feast on a variety of insects such as aphids, flies, mosquitoes, caterpillars, and beetles. However, the ones sold in most garden centers are the Asian variety, not native to North America. Additionally, praying mantids will not target just the "pest" insects within your garden—they are known to annihilate any insect they meet, including precious pollinators, and even small birds like hummingbirds. When you think about it, adding egg sacs full of nonnative bugs capable of mass destruction might not be the best course of action when trying to balance the garden ecosystem! This same care should be taken when buying beneficial insects of any variety: We have to be mindful of the unintended consequences of disrupting the natural ecosystem and instead find ways to support its ability to keep pests in check.

A convergent ladybug, native to North America, moves in to feed on an aphid on a sweet pea.

Nematodes. These worms are a vital part of the soil food web, and some are considered beneficial for pest control (though others, such as root knot nematodes, *Meloidogyne* species, are considered pests). Many beneficial nematodes are available; they are often targeted to specific pest larvae, especially Japanese beetles, flea beetles, thrips, and the white grubs commonly found in lawns.

This tray of snapdragon seedlings in soil blocks is ready for planting; the seedlings' robust root systems help the plants resist pest pressure.

They sound like a great option for taking care of pests, with no damage or harm done to humans, right? And it's true—beneficial insects and nematodes are less damaging to the garden overall than pesticides. However, I do not use them in my own garden. Why not?

Beneficial nematodes sold at nurseries are not necessarily native species, and even if the species of nematode is native, the subspecies may not be. Typically, they are sold in mixes of various types meant to target a range of pests. Given the dangers of invasive pests such as lantern flies, Japanese beetles, jumping worms, and more, we should always consider the potential for invasive insects to take hold in our gardens and be wary of introducing any, "beneficial" or not, that may damage native populations.

Whenever possible, I avoid artificially impacting the pest population in my garden by purchasing insects because it can be difficult to know how those imports interfere with the natural balance. The goal of the regenerative garden is not to artificially create or purchase a healthy environment for plants but to establish one through practices and plantings.

Remember: There is no quick fix! Gardening with nature is a process to embrace and not one to rush.

Plants from Nurseries

What are the most frequently purchased garden items? The plants themselves. Many of us simply don't have the time to start our entire garden from seed, and that is completely understandable. But there are lots of considerations when it comes to bringing store-bought plants into the garden, and reasons why purchased plants are not always the best option for the ecologically focused regenerative garden.

Questions to Ask at the Nursery When Buying Plants

Were these plants grown on-site from seed, or were they grown from plugs? Many nurseries don't grow from seed but rather purchase smaller plugs and grow the plants larger, or they buy fully grown plants at wholesale prices that they then resell. If they do not grow from seed, it becomes more difficult to know what the plants were treated with before you purchase them, because the plants may have gone through two or three nurseries prior to your bringing them home.

Can you provide a list of everything these plants were treated with? When you ask this, the employees will likely look at you like you have two heads. If they can't answer this question, ask for a manager to provide a detailed list of the treatments the plants received during their growing. If they are unable (or unwilling) to provide this, let them know that you would be happy to purchase from them in the future if, and when, they are able to provide this information.

What to look for: Be on the lookout for systemic pesticides in particular: neonicotinoids like imidacloprid, and other systemic herbicides or fungicides. There are lots of them. This is part of the reason I prefer growing from seed: I know what's gone into my plants before I put them into my garden. Some of the treatments are relatively harmless, while others can be more nefarious. When in doubt, look up the chemical treatments used.

How long have these plants been in trays, and do the roots need loosening before planting? Ideally, the nursery employee will assist you by pulling a seedling gently out of its tray to help you inspect the roots for the appearance of circling. A telltale sign is if the seedling is very difficult to remove or you see roots exiting the bottom of the container, or if the seedling container is very firm to a gentle squeeze, which can indicate excessive root circling and density (see Healthier Seedlings, page 74).

This root-bound seedling was planted in spring and pulled out in fall. See how the roots have continued to circle and girdle themselves, barely allowing for growth and leading to drought sensitivity and poor performance.

KNOW YOUR PLANT HISTORIES

It's important to know the history of the plants you purchase for your garden. Until five years ago, I bought small plants, called plugs, that were grown by an offsite nursery. Using pre-grown plants is an easy way to start a garden, but it can create problems and challenges later on. I started questioning the plant industry after listening to a podcast detailing the Xerces Society's research about systemic pesticides found in nursery stock. When I contacted our plug supplier to ask what was being applied on the seedlings I ordered, I was given a list of fungicides and pesticides used to ensure the health of plugs grown on a greenhouse production scale. This included a systemic fungicide containing boscalid and pyraclostrobin, which some early studies indicate can negatively impact survival and queen production in honeybees and impair nest recognition in solitary bees. I was incredibly disappointed—but as I've learned, this is to be expected in the land of nursery-grown plants.

The sad reality is that most plants are not grown from seed on-site. Some smaller nurseries may still grow from seed, or grow a percentage of their plants from seed, but the majority buy them as plugs, pot them into larger containers, and sell them. In fact, some plants are germinated at one nursery, sent to another nursery to grow out, then sent to a third nursery to grow out even further before being shipped to the customer or final nursery.

AVOID CONTAMINATION WITH PESTICIDES

Many seedlings travel umpteen miles before landing in their final garden home, and along the way they face many different opportunities for pesticides and fungicides to be applied, unbeknownst to the gardener. These pesticides can include the infamous neonicotinoids, a class of systemic pesticide that not only kills pollinators visiting the treated plants but also stays in the tissue of the plant for months to years, killing pollinators that visit its flowers for extended periods.

A study published in *Biological Conservation* revealed concerning levels of pesticides in milkweed plants obtained from retail nurseries across the United States. Pesticide contamination was detected in *all* tested milkweed plants, raising concerns for conservation efforts aimed at protecting monarch butterflies, whose larvae rely on milkweed as their sole food source. The study collected 235 milkweed leaf samples from nurseries in 15 states and uncovered a total of 61 different pesticides, with an average of 12—and up to 28—per plant. While only a fraction of the chemicals detected have been tested for their impacts on monarchs, 38 percent of the samples contained residue levels potentially harmful to monarchs' migration and foraging abilities, primarily due to the elevated fungicide levels. Interestingly, plants labeled as "wildlife-friendly" did not necessarily have fewer pesticide residues; in some cases, their levels were even higher.

To guarantee plants' safety for pollinators and other insects integral to our garden ecosystem, it's essential that we seek out absolutely safe plant sources—or, even better, start plants ourselves from seed for full transparency into how they were grown and what they were treated with. That way, we know that these plants are safe to use as the foundation of our garden's food web.

HEALTHIER SEEDLINGS

Here's another benefit of growing from seed: It often results in healthier seedlings *and* adult plants that are more likely to ward off insect damage and are less susceptible to drought and disease. Many plants in the nursery have been in containers for too long and start to outgrow their pots, leading to root-bound plants with roots circling inside their plastic pots. While bound roots can be partially untangled before planting, a good amount of circling continues as the plants grow in the ground, leading to roots that suffocate each other and struggle to reach deeply into the soil to get enough water and nutrients. When you grow from seed, you can ensure seedlings are planted at the optimal time.

A monarch, an example of a specialist pollinator, feeds on the nectar from a milkweed plant.

Using Pesticides (More) Safely

I truly hope that after reading this book, you understand how using pesticides, even organic ones that may claim to be safe, can impact the complicated workings of a garden ecosystem and be incredibly detrimental to the goals of the regenerative garden. However, if you choose to use any, please follow these tips to protect pollinators as much as possible.

Exhaust all other options first. Attempt manually removing pests, using insect netting, and evaluating your garden ecosystem before using any sort of pesticide.

Read all labels thoroughly (and then read some more). Go beyond what's simply on the label and do your own research on any product you choose to use.

Properly identify insects. Confirm which insects are doing the damage that you intend to target. If you are simply guessing, you may target the wrong insect, which can cause more harm than good. If you can't find what is munching on your plants during the day, try going out at night with a flashlight—damage is often done under the cover of darkness.

Do not treat flowering plants. Treating flowering plants may lead to contaminated pollen and nectar. For instance, azadirachtin, the active ingredient in neem oil, has been shown to damage larval populations of bumblebees that partake in such contaminated food sources. Products such as neem oil may tell you that applying at dusk is safe, but we know from our own garden experiences that bumblebees and beneficial insects are often present at these hours, even sleeping overnight on the underside of blooms like zinnias and bee balm.

Protect pollinators. Do not apply pesticides where any pollinators are foraging (remember, moths are pollinators, too).

Minimize herbicide use. Whenever possible, remove weeds by hand or keep them mowed down to prevent weed spread as an alternative to spraying herbicide. If an herbicide must be used on invasive trees or shrubs, cut into the cambium and paint the herbicide on the cut instead of spraying the plant, an approach that is safer for pollinators and soil (see page 110).

Choose products with short half-lives. If insecticides absolutely must be applied during the flowering period, choose ones with the shortest half-lives. Neonicotinoids such as imidacloprid are highly toxic to pollinators and can remain in plant tissues for months to years. Anything with such a long half-life should be avoided at all costs. And watch out, as these insecticides can even be mixed in with some ornamental fertilizers.

Do not apply any pesticide in windy conditions. The spray or powder can drift onto plants and blooms you don't intend it to reach. Also, if spraying, decrease the pressure of your sprayer to help reduce potential drifting.

A bumblebee rests on a Palmer's penstemon at dusk.

Seed Starting in the Regenerative Garden

Avoiding waste and potential contamination, including with plastic seed trays and peat-based seed-starting soils, is essential to the regenerative garden. The peat-based soils used in most plastic seed-starting trays come with a heavy environmental footprint, and plastic clearly has its own disadvantages. While it is possible, of course, to grow healthy plants using conventional plastic trays, there are downsides.

Plastic seed trays and pots are not always recyclable and often have a limited life. With exposure to sunlight, even the strong ones eventually wear down, crack, and break. Even if black plastic is recyclable in your area, much of the plastic waste we send to recycling centers isn't actually recycled, and it still requires petroleum to produce.

Plastics, including recycled plastics, can potentially work their way into your garden soil. Plastic containers have been shown to leach chemicals into their contents, especially in moist and warm conditions. Various studies have revealed that phthalates, bisphenol A (BPA), and other additives commonly found in plastics can migrate into the surrounding environment.

Seed-starting trays made of recycled plastics are also not ideal—new research shows that recycled plastic leaches more toxic chemicals than virgin plastic. According to a study in 2023, heating plastics during recycling can produce additional harmful chemicals, such as the carcinogen benzene, that can contaminate the recycled materials. The plastic recycling process itself leaches substantial quantities of microplastics into the water supply as the plastics are ground down and re-formed.

Much research on the impacts of plastics is still being conducted, but from what we know now, this gardener just does not believe that the continued use of plastic seed-starting trays is best for the planet or our gardens. The good news is, there's an excellent reusable alternative, made of metal, that creates more vigorous and healthful plants: It's called a soil blocker.

Soil-blocked seedlings from our greenhouse sit outside to harden off before planting. The blocks are held in fiberglass cafeteria trays, which last decades at a minimum.

After a soil block is formed, it is ready to be seeded into.

These soil-blocked peppers have a robust root system and are ready for planting.

Soil Blocking: A Plastic-Free Alternative

Soil blocking entails making cubes of soil and planting seeds into those cubes instead of in seed trays. The cubes are formed with a soil blocker—a metal frame with a plunger system that compresses and cuts soil into blocks. The metal frame is pressed into wet soil mix, which is then plunged out onto a tray, resulting in perfect cubes of soil. If the soil mix is made correctly, the blocks do not crumble as easily as you might think, and the blocks become structurally sound as the plant roots spread into the soil.

Rather than using plastic trays to hold our soil blocks, we put our blocks into low-sided fiberglass trays (ours are cafeteria trays we salvaged from a restaurant that was closing, but they can be purchased online), which have the potential to last decades with good care. No items need repurchasing after the initial investment in materials, so you save money in just a couple of seasons. These are flat-bottomed trays with no drainage holes; water can be gently poured alongside the blocks, which wick the water up, and any excess can be poured off the side.

THE BENEFITS OF SOIL BLOCKING

The advantages of soil blocking, beyond the reduction of plastic use, are many. They make the time to learn this method more than worthwhile.

Space saving. This method can conserve space, creating room for more seedlings and taking up less room for storage. Soil blocks can be packed more densely onto a flat-bottomed tray because they lack the separators between cells found in plastic seed trays. Once seedlings have been planted, the fiberglass trays pack flat, and there are no bulky seed trays to store.

Stronger roots. Because soil blocks are exposed to air on the sides, the plant's roots become "air pruned"; that is, rather than continuing to grow around the edges of a container, the roots hit the air and stop, just as they do in nature (air pruning is the reason you'll never see roots growing up into the air out of the ground). This results in a seedling that, when planted, is ready to explode outward into the surrounding soil, seeking nutrients and water for growth and establishing the deep roots needed to withstand drought.

Less transplant shock. One major perk of soil blocking is that the rate of transplant shock—a major cause of plant loss in spring—is greatly reduced. Transplant shock occurs at planting time, when a seedling is removed from its container and its roots are loosened and planted out. Soil block–grown seedlings are significantly more immune to transplant shock because their roots are jostled much less.

Easier to plant. Planting soil blocks is fuss-free. There are no seed trays to awkwardly wrestle with to remove your seedlings: Just gently pull apart the blocks if roots have grown into neighboring blocks, then moisten with water or compost tea (see page 186).

Some gardeners find that there is a learning curve to soil blocking; but after several tries, most are converted by the healthier, more vigorous seedlings they plant in spring.

The off-season storage needs of a soil blocker and flat trays are minimal.

MAKING SOIL BLOCKS

Soil blocks are very easy to make in just a few steps. The key is getting the soil moisture level right: You'll want it more moist than a typical seed-starting medium, but not sloppy!

MATERIALS

- Seed starting mix (see page 85) or potting soil
- ¼-inch mesh sifter (optional, depending on soil mix)
- Flat-bottom bin for mixing and pressing the soil mix
- Metal bench scraper or putty knife for mixing soil and scraping off the soil blocker to create flat block bottoms (Alternatively, use your hands.)
- Soil blocker (I prefer the medium-size blocker, which makes five 1½-inch soil blocks at one time and is the best size for learning the method. The smaller blocks dry out quickly, and the large ones take up an unnecessary amount of space and can crumble more easily.)
- Trays with flat bottoms, such as fiberglass cafeteria trays
- Humidity dome (You can use plastic wrap or a beeswax wrap made with cotton fabric and beeswax pastilles if you want to avoid plastic.)

1. Make the seed-starting mix. There are various recipes out there for soil blocks, but many of them use the generic term *compost* as a component, and composts can be difficult to assess. If you prefer to use a bagged potting soil for soil blocking, you can, but try to source a peat-free option; it may take some experimenting to find the best one for you.
2. If using potting soil, I recommend sifting the soil before forming your blocks to remove any chunks or sticks from the mixture and create a more even consistency. This will ensure the most success with your blocks.
3. Combine the soil mixture with warm (not hot) water in the bin. The amount of water needed will vary depending on how moist your soil is out of the bag; generally, a bit of water should be left in the bottom of the bin when you run a bench scraper across it. If you pick up a handful of mix and squeeze, some water should run out from between your fingers, but it should not be overly wet—think glistening.
4. Ideally, let the mix sit overnight for best incorporation.
5. Press the soil blocker into the soil mix, wiggling the blocker back and forth and repeating until the blocker is full of soil.
6. Scrape the bottom of the blocker with the scraper, and repeat step 5.
7. After the second press and scrape, move the blocker to the tray.
8. Depress and gently lift up the blocker to press out the soil blocks.
9. Place seeds directly into the soil blocks and cover to keep in humidity as needed, depending on the seed type.
10. When watering soil blocks, be sure to bottom water gently around the blocks, allowing it to wick up, rather than pour water on top. Gently pour off any excess water that isn't wicked up within a few minutes to avoid root rot.
11. Fertilizing needs for plants started in soil blocks will be similar to plants grown in trays, although our soil blocking mix is a bit richer than most standard seed-starting recipes, especially if you include the wool pellets.

1. *Make the soil mix.*

2. *Sift mix if necessary to remove large chunks.*

3. *Add water to achieve correct consistency.*

4. *Stir the mix to wet and incorporate all ingredients thoroughly.*

5. *Press the soil blocker into the mix.*

6. *Scrape blocker for a level base.*

7. *Move blocker to tray.*

8. *Depress and lift blocker.*

9. *Plant seeds.*

Soil blocks can be made from a variety of soils and ingredients. Recipes vary, but we recommend avoiding peat if possible and turning to alternatives such as coconut coir, worm castings, and vermiculite, as seen here.

MATERIALS FOR YOUR SOIL BLOCKING MIXTURE

Not every seed-starting soil works for soil blocking, and many seed-starting soils are sterile and devoid of nutrients—long thought to be a good thing, but we've found our seedlings do much better with some nutrients in the mix. There are many soil blocking recipes available, but most list a generic "compost" as a component. Compost can range widely in ingredients and quality, and for seed starting, a well-balanced homemade compost will yield much better results than a purchased manure-based one, for example. For this reason, we developed the following peat-free soil block recipe using coconut coir, worm castings, and vermiculite, which are all readily available. Worm castings can either be purchased or made at home by starting a worm bin and vermicomposting (see page 182).

If you have access to wool pellets (a by-product of wool shearing), you can add them for some additional slow-release nitrogen, but they are not strictly necessary. To make it easier to incorporate the wool pellets into the mix, we add water to them to make them a loose, slurry-like consistency first. If you use the wool pellets, you will likely be able to skip fertilizing your seedlings as they grow; without it, a weekly dose of fish emulsion (1 teaspoon per gallon) will be beneficial once seedlings have two sets of leaves.

Mix wool pellets with water to create a loose, slurry-like texture before adding it to your soil blocking mix.

The Problem with Peat (and Some Sustainable Alternatives)

Most store-bought seed-starting and potting soils available in the United States contain peat (though it is banned for use in garden products in the UK, Ireland, and the Netherlands due to ecological concerns). Peat has very few nutrients but is often used due to its light texture and ability to retain moisture.

I do not use peat products here at the farm; while some in the garden industry maintain that peat is environmentally friendly to use, we choose to seek out alternatives. Peat bogs sequester about 25 percent of the globe's soil carbon (twice the amount of carbon sequestered by forested areas), despite covering only 3 percent of the earth's surface. Harvesting peat from bogs for use as a soil amendment releases carbon dioxide rather than storing it, as peat does in its natural state. To harvest peat, the bogs must first be drained, decimating a delicate ecosystem, and it regrows slowly—at a rate of only about 0.04 inch per year—meaning that even the efforts to regrow harvested bogs can't keep up with the harvesting. Research estimates that emissions from drained or burned peatlands account for 5 percent of all greenhouse gas emissions caused by human activity. The UK banned the sale of peat to home gardeners in 2024 due to these impacts.

In addition to the ecological concerns, I dislike how peat acts as a seed-starting or container soil: Lightweight and prone to wind erosion, it's also very difficult to rewet once dry. There are alternatives to peat, including the following.

Rehydrated compressed coconut coir is a more sustainable alternative to peat.

COCONUT COIR

Coconut coir is a widely available alternative, though it comes with its own set of issues, including questionable labor practices, high water usage in processing to mitigate the material's salinity, and travel distance to reach the northern hemisphere. However, it is still a better option than peat, as it is a secondary-use material (it is derived from the husks of coconuts being processed for their water and meat) and would otherwise be a waste product. It often comes as a compressed cube that needs to be soaked in water prior to use. It is basically devoid of nutrients and therefore can be used interchangeably with peat.

WOOL

Wool pellets are made of compressed sheep's wool, often from the seconds, or wool unsuitable for fabric production that would otherwise be discarded. We have experimented extensively with wool pellets as a peat alternative and have found them to be incredibly useful in soil blocking. Like peat, they retain water well, but they also contain a slow-release nitrogen.

Wool pellets are not widely used yet and can therefore be expensive. In our experience, unprocessed raw wool doesn't work well for soil blocking (it tends to stay together as long fibers, which are difficult to press into cubes). However, it can serve as an alternative to wool pellets when used as a bottom lining material in flat wooden trays. If you use it this way, beware of invasive weed seeds that can be carried in unprocessed wool, and vet your sources. If you are concerned about animal welfare, ask questions of your wool source to ensure that the sheep are being treated humanely, but know that sheep must be shorn of their wool as part of humane practices.

LEAF MOLD

We have experimented with homemade leaf mold but haven't yet found quite the right ratio to use it for seed starting. In our experience, it can rob nitrogen from young seedlings if not fully "finished." However, it is a wonderful alternative to peat if you are adding it to the garden soil directly! It contributes organic matter to soil and aerates sandy and clay soils. Leaf mold can contain some nutrients (more than peat) and aids in water retention.

Coconut coir, wool pellets, and leaf mold are all good alternatives to peat; which one you use will depend on your personal values and on the seeds you start. For example, I have found that seeds that prefer dryer and less rich conditions, such as plants native to my area, did not like the higher nutrient density and water-retaining qualities of wool, so I do not use it for those plants.

When using wooden trays, spreading a layer of raw wool in the bottom provides nutrients and helps prevent leaking.

A handful of finished leaf mold makes another excellent homemade alternative to peat.

MY GO-TO SEED-STARTING RECIPE

This recipe works equally well in wooden trays (see page 86) or any seed-starting tray. If you have access to raw, unpelletized wool, you can use it to line the bottom of your wooden seed trays in lieu of using the wool pellets. The wool will absorb excess water and provide slow-release nitrogen to the seedlings once their roots reach the bottom.

Note: This recipe is by volume, not weight. It doesn't matter if you measure with a mason jar or a bucket; use what you have. You can also mix this with any old leftover seed-starting mix or potting soil you have around and need to use up.

MATERIALS

- 4 cups coconut coir
- 6 cups worm castings (can be purchased in bags or made in a worm compost bin at home; see page 182)
- 4 cups vermiculite
- 1 tablespoon mycorrhizae
- Optional: 1 cup wool pellets, mixed with equal parts water after measuring to help facilitate breakdown
- 3 cups warm water

Mix the coconut coir, worm castings, vermiculite, mycorrhizae, and wool pellets (if using), then add enough of the water to reach the desired consistency.

If purchasing multiple ingredients for a seed-starting recipe is daunting to you, you can use a store-bought potting soil as the medium. We recommend a high-quality, peat-free potting soil, sifted through a ¼-inch sifter to remove large chunks.

Mix the seed-starting ingredients.

Coconut coir is used instead of peat.

Add water and combine.

Starting Seeds in Wooden Trays

Soil blocking is not for everyone; it takes time to form and carefully water the blocks. So another plastic-free seed-starting method uses wooden seed trays you assemble from upcycled scrap lumber or cedar. This requires an investment of time up front but saves more in the long run. We made our first wooden seed trays from cedar lumber sourced from old discarded raised beds and have also made them from discarded untreated cedar fencing.

While many folks are surprised to see wooden trays, an older generation remembers when they were the standard, before plastic became the cheaper and more convenient solution. Nurseries that grew in wooden trays would scoop out seedlings and package them in newspaper to send home with customers.

These days, fears about leaking and rot are the concerns we most often hear about wooden trays. Leaking can occur if the trays are overwatered, so we carefully overhead water to moisten the soil and avoid wet floors. And yes, wood will rot with continued exposure to moisture, but by letting trays dry out between uses, we extend their life significantly.

They can also be treated by means of the traditional Japanese waterproofing technique called shou sugi ban (see Shou Sugi Ban, page 90). This method involves charring the surface of the wood and then sealing it with raw linseed oil or beeswax, creating a natural barrier against moisture and pests without the need for harmful chemicals. Note: Only raw linseed oil is food safe.

BENEFITS OF WOODEN TRAYS

There are many reasons to use wooden planting trays. Well-made wooden trays should last a decade or more with good care. If DIY isn't your cup of tea, you can source cedar trays online.

Environmental benefits. Wood is a renewable resource, unlike plastic, which is derived from fossil fuels. Wooden trays are biodegradable and can be composted at the end of their life cycle.

Excellent water retention. Because a soil-filled tray functions as one large planting space (versus many separate containers), it retains moisture quite well, meaning it requires less frequent watering and attention.

Fast to fill. All you need to do is mix your soil, moisten it, and pour it into the trays. I go one step further and divide the soil into sections using a putty knife. This step is optional, but it can be helpful for spacing seedlings evenly and when transplanting.

Custom sizing. You can make these trays any size you'd like. Ours are fairly large because we start lots of seeds, but that comes with the downside of being heavy when full of wet soil. At home, you might want to start with smaller seed trays. When choosing what size to build them to, consider the size of your seed-starting area and shelving to maximize space.

Aesthetics. If you prefer a more natural-looking garden space, you will love the earthy quality of wooden seed trays, which evoke a woodsy, heirloom feel, especially if made with salvaged wood.

Wooden trays are a plastic-free method for starting seeds. If well cared for, the trays can last a decade or more.

BUILDING AND USING **WOODEN TRAYS**

Follow these tips for building your own DIY biodegradable wooden seed trays.

TOOLS

- Saw
- Drill
- Garden knife or box scraper
- Large spoon

MATERIALS

- 8 to 10 wood scraps, 2 × 4-inch or similar, depending on desired box size (I prefer to source untreated salvaged cedar from old fencing or raised beds or heat-treated pallets. Avoid painted wood or pressure-treated lumber from before 2003, when arsenic was used in treatment.)
- Wood screws (20 per tray)
- Seed-starting mix (see page 85)

OPTIONAL (IF TREATING WITH SHOU SUGI BAN)

- Butane or propane torch
- Stiff-bristled brush
- Raw linseed oil or beeswax/raw linseed oil blend

1. Using a saw, cut the wood for the seed trays to the dimensions you chose based on your seed-starting space.
2. Drill pilot holes to avoid splitting the wood.
3. Attach the pieces with wood screws. Add handles made from scrap wood to allow for lifting.
4. Place wool in the tray if using.
5. To fill, gently press soil into the tray. Carefully pour water to further moisten the soil if needed.
6. Using the putty knife, mark the soil into sections.
7. Press the seeds into the soil and cover as needed, depending on the seed type.
8. Top-water to moisten the seedlings until they are ready for transplanting.
9. To transplant, scoop out a seedling and the surrounding soil with a spoon and move the seedling to a planting hole.

Optional: Preserve wooden tray using shou sugi ban method (see Shou Sugi Ban, page 90).

1. *Precut or gather scrap wood boards.*

2. *Drill pilot holes to avoid splitting the wood.*

3. *Attach the pieces with a drill and wood screws.*

4. *Place wool in the tray.*

5. *Cover with soil.*

5. *Moisten soil.*

6. *Use a garden knife or sharp tool to mark the soil into sections.*

7. *Plant seeds.*

9. *Scoop the seedlings out with a spoon.*

Shou Sugi Ban

I often hear that "wood will just rot," but this is not necessarily true. If you want your wood to last longer, you can seal and preserve it using the Japanese process of shou sugi ban, also known as yakisugi. Here at the farm, I treat my wooden seed trays and wooden garden beds with this method to eliminate the need for plastic liners and make them last a long time. Avoid using this technique near flammable surfaces, and be sure to have a water source close by in case of accidental flare-ups.

1. *Place the cedar seed-starting tray on a nonflammable surface.*

2. *Using a handheld butane or propane torch, char the wood long enough to achieve char or alligatored surface.*

3. *Use a stiff-bristled brush to brush off loose char.*

4. *Seal by rubbing on a food-safe oil. We use a blend of beeswax and raw linseed oil, which provides extra longevity. The wood can be re-oiled if you notice that water no longer beads up on the surface.*

More Options for Reducing Plastic in the Regenerative Garden

There are many unexpected materials containing plastic that can work their way into your garden. To avoid introducing plastic materials, keep an eye out for these products and try replacing them with their plastic-free alternatives.

Sneaky Sources of Plastic in the Regenerative Garden	Alternatives (See Retailers and Nurseries, page 207)
Seed trays (often made of plastic, or worse, recycled plastic, which contains more chemicals and puts billions of microplastics into the water during the recycling process)	Soil blockers, wooden trays, other upcycled containers
Grow bags (typically made of polyester and recycled plastic)—fabrics are even bigger sources of microplastic contamination due to fabric's propensity to shed	Wool bags, hemp bags, upcycled burlap (such as coffee bags)
Plant tags	Wooden tags or popsicle sticks, metal labels
Netting	Jute netting, cotton, wool yarn, hemp
Plastic landscape mulch (a.k.a. landscape fabric)	Cover crops grown as mulch, organic mulches
Plastic pots	Terra cotta, ceramic
Frost fabric (typically made of spun bonded polypropylene)	100% cotton cover
Shade cloth	Burlap
Insect netting	100% cotton cover
PVC piping for hoops	Electrical metal conduit bent with hoop bender

4

Build Your Soil Armor

NO MATTER HOW BUSY I GET ON THE FARM, I always make time to mulch my beds. I think of mulch as a kind of soil armor, because it protects and serves the soil food web in so many ways. Over the years, we have found that our garden is healthiest where we use mulch. Soil organisms rely on consistent soil conditions. Mulch moderates the soil surface temperature (shielding it from both heat and extreme cold), maintains soil moisture, and provides organic matter to help feed the soil life, all of which are essential to the soil food web.

Weed Management with Natural Mulching

Not only is mulch beneficial for the soil food web and the health of the garden as a whole, it is also the key to weed management in regenerative gardening; the thicker the layer of mulch, the more it limits weed growth. We now rely solely on various types of mulches for our weed strategy at the farm, though that's not how we started out!

Moving Away from Landscape Fabric

When we started the farm, I did what most other farmers in my area were doing, and what was most recommended online, which was using black landscape "fabric" (which isn't a true fabric but rather a woven polypropylene). While this is a valid way to prevent weeds, especially on a large scale, it also has its disadvantages, especially from a regenerative and ecological standpoint.

HOW LANDSCAPING FABRIC WORKS

I'll pause here to note that the way farmers and gardeners use landscape fabric is not how the product is typically used in home and commercial landscaping, where the fabric is placed down and then topped with mulch. That use is just silly, as over time organic matter breaks down on top of the fabric and weeds end up growing on and through the fabric anyway, leaving you with a mess in your landscape!

These sweet peas on a trellis are mulched to keep roots cool.

The soil around this fall asparagus is mulched with straw.

The way farmers and many gardeners use landscape fabric is quite different: With a propane or butane torch, the farmer burns holes in the fabric in a grid pattern for the plants to grow through, and the fabric is placed on top of the soil with no mulch covering it. Typically the fabric is stapled down for the growing season and removed and stored in the offseason until spring planting.

PLASTICS AND SOIL HEALTH

We completely stopped using landscape fabric as a mulch two seasons ago. (It's now sitting in our storage shed, waiting for a recycling opportunity.) I regret ever using it. When I began understanding how vital soil ecology is to the health of our gardens and the planet, and that petrochemicals are used to produce polypropylene, I dove into research on the fabric's impacts on soil. A shocking report on agricultural plastic use was issued by the United Nations' Food and Agriculture Organization in 2021 in which the director stated that "soils are one of the main receptors of agricultural plastics and are known to contain larger quantities of microplastics than oceans."

I became increasingly concerned after seeing the fabric degradation that occurred in our beds, despite the material being rated for 20 years of use: Staple tears and other wear resulted in pieces ripping off into the field, and birds would pick up these pieces to use in their nests. We could see the macroplastics in the soil, which we now know break down over time into invisible micro- and nanoplastics.

Numerous studies have indicated that microplastics negatively affect the soil food web by disrupting nutrient cycling, altering microbial communities, and impairing the health and reproduction of soil organisms. Plants can take up microplastics through their roots, and those particles can end up in the produce we eat. So with every year that I let that plastic sit and slowly break down, baking in the hot sun on moist soil, I was damaging the very soil life I was trying to nurture. It continues to surprise me that woven plastic mulches are allowed in organic food production, and it is one of the main reasons I started growing more of my family's food myself.

PLASTICS IN THE LANDFILL

While plastic can be a huge time-saver for many farmers, both for occultation and as a mulch, there are insufficient recycling options, and after its useful life is over, the reality is that it ends up in the landfill with the remainder of our world's rapidly accumulating plastic.

At my farm, we now use natural mulches in all our gardens and fields. In doing side-by-side microscopic tests on soil under landscape fabric and soil under natural mulches, I found that there were significantly higher rates of fungi, microbes, and nematodes in the soil under the natural mulch, and none of the compaction and cracked soil I would often find after removing fabric at the end of a season.

A shred of landscape fabric has been picked up by a bird and used in a nest.

Leaves make excellent mulch and are readily available in many home landscapes.

To protect beds over the winter, cover them with a generous layer of leaves. Only use leaves that have not been treated with pesticides or raked up with noxious weeds and seeds.

Mulch Options in the Regenerative Garden

There are so many natural mulching options—which should you choose? In my garden, I like to use whatever is free and abundant—typically that includes dead garden plants, leaves, pine needles, and wood chips. Remember, part of the goal of regenerative gardening is closing waste loops, so start with what's most readily available to *you* and what has to travel the fewest miles to reach your garden.

Leaves

Because of how easy they are to find, leaves from deciduous trees are one of my favorite mulches. They are abundant in many regions and often can be obtained easily and for free. Each year at the farm, I run a leaf donation program, gathering hundreds of bags of leaves from the community to mulch our fall fields. This makes mulching so simple: The leaves have already been raked and bagged, and all we have to do is dump them where we want them! I recommend using leaves from a wide array of tree types to mitigate any potential negative allelopathy, such as can occur with black walnut leaves. Not only does leaf mulch support nesting insects (and in turn, bird populations), it also breaks down quickly into soil, becoming beautiful humus.

If wind is an issue, burlap placed over the top of the leaves and weighed down with bricks or other heavy items will help keep them in place.

Once we've spread leaves over the soil for winter protection, we store extra leaves in makeshift leaf towers (see page 169) for spring applications, when the leaves make an excellent mulch for actively growing plants. While mowing or chopping the leaves is a popular option, I prefer not to mow or chop in fall or early spring so as to not disturb any nesting members of our soil food web hiding within them! Once soil temperatures have warmed consistently in late spring, feel free to chop the leaves. Any pollinators or nesting insects likely have emerged by that point.

Be sure to use leaves from trees that have not been sprayed or treated with any kind of

Pine needles make great mulch for plants that prefer drier soil, like these lisianthus.

pesticide or raked from ground with any noxious weeds that could contaminate your garden soil.

Best for: Mulching garden beds in fall and providing habitat for beneficial insects; or chopping into finer pieces in late spring and using as a mulch around annuals.

Pine Needles

The first year at the farm, I turned away a beautiful truckload of raked pine needles from a landscaper and have been kicking myself since learning what an excellent mulch they make!

For a long time, I believed the myth that pine needles make soil acidic, so I was scared to use them on my garden beds. Once we finally tried them out, I was delighted at how well they worked—they didn't blow away like leaves did, were easy and lightweight to spread, had a pleasant pine smell, and mulched young seedlings perfectly because the fine shade cast by the needles didn't suffocate tiny baby plants like heavier mulches would, allowing me to mulch the young plants earlier. The pine needles didn't harbor as many earwigs as wood chip mulch seemed to, and I had abundant needles available from my parents, who live on a wooded mountain lot and rake their needles annually as part of wildfire mitigation practices.

Pine needles (sometimes called pine straw) were long assumed to create acidic soil because it's difficult to grow plants underneath pines—but this is a misunderstanding. In reality, plants struggle under pine trees because the area is typically shady and dry, and most plants don't thrive in that environment. If anything, pine needles on the surface of the soil barely affect the soil pH (unless you layer on feet of them or a great deal are worked into the soil), because decomposing organisms neutralize the acidity of pine needles. So go ahead and incorporate pine needles into your mulching routine if you have access to them, without fears of acidic soil!

Best for: Annuals, perennials, or biennials. Because pine needles are slower to decompose than leaves or straw, they may not break down in one season. I use them around annuals that prefer drier soil because they don't form as thick a mat as leaves do.

Wood chips make great mulch for perennials, on paths and walkways, and to prep new areas for planting.

Fresh ramial wood chips—those made from small to medium branches and leaves—have a higher ratio of cambium (inner bark), which contains more nutrients than heartwood or sapwood.

Wood Chips

I first want to clarify what material I'm referencing when talking about wood chip mulch. This is not the dyed brown, red, or black "mulch" available in plastic bags from the big-box stores. The dyes in those mulches, while typically safe, can hide materials that you do not want in your garden soil, such as chunks of lumber reclaimed from construction projects that could potentially contain chemicals. Instead, it is best to seek out wood chips from a local tree service, who will provide fresh tree chips. See someone doing tree trimming in your neighborhood? Pop over and ask if they'll dump the chips at your driveway when they're done (they're usually all too happy to not have to haul them far!), or sign up for a free chip drop.

I like getting a couple of loads of wood chips delivered in late summer when the trees are still leafed out. The leaves in the mixture provide a nitrogen source to balance the carbon in the wood, heating the pile and helping it break down, in effect creating a wood chip compost pile. We let the pile sit over winter, and by spring the pile's heat has decomposed the material slightly for a finer wood chip with lots of fungal mycelium in it.

Best for: I prefer using wood chips and other heavy mulches that take a long time to break down around perennial plants and trees, in paths and walkways, and to prep new areas for planting.

Here, pathways are mulched with a mix of leaves, straw, wood chips, and other organic material, depending on what's available.

Straw mulch shades the soil, helps retain moisture, and reduces weed seed germination.

Straw

At our family home farm in Minnesota, we have an entire gigantic haymow full to the brim of beautiful herbicide-free straw that's nearing 50 years old now. (It was put into the barn in 1977, the last year my grandpa was able to farm the land before succumbing to emphysema.) I would *love* to have that mulch for my garden! Unfortunately, it's a thousand miles away from my home farm, but if I could put it all in a truck and move it, I would!

Straw can be an excellent garden mulch. Lightweight, easy to spread, and readily available for most, it creates a nice dry surface for the plants (ideal to hold off disease) while keeping the soil shaded and moist.

Unless you know for sure that store-bought straw is herbicide-free, it's best to age it before adding it to your garden beds. This gives any herbicides time to break down and dissipate. Here I've mulched a path with straw and manure from spent animal bedding to decompose and age in place before shoveling it onto an adjacent bed the following season.

STRAW VERSUS HAY

It's common for a small amount of grass (like timothy) to sprout from straw, because it's difficult to harvest it 100 percent clean of seeds—but to avoid a garden *full* of grass, be sure to select straw, and not hay, which has many more seeds!

Best for: Mulching around annuals to retain moisture and reduce weed germination.

Herbicide Contamination in Straw

Unfortunately, modern agricultural practices result in much available straw being contaminated with herbicides. As farms battle increasingly aggressive weeds (one consequence of the frequent use of herbicide is herbicide-resistant weeds), the herbicides being used are more persistent and increasingly harsh. Broadleaf pesticides, such as picloram, clopyralid, and aminopyralid, are frequently applied, and residues can remain present on straw for months to years afterward.

I've seen gardeners unknowingly use straw mulch contaminated with herbicide and have their entire plot ruined for years—by the time the symptoms are seen in the plants, the chemicals are often leached into the soil. Unless you can get a guarantee from your straw provider that there is no contamination of any herbicides, I wouldn't trust straw bales as garden mulch, personally—it is too risky.

If you do have straw and aren't sure whether it's safe to use, there are a couple options for you. One is to do a test patch of a quick-germinating and -growing plant such as radish or turnip and mulch it with the straw. If the seedling yellows or the leaves curl as it germinates and grows, indicating herbicide contamination, the straw is a no-go. Or you can try our method when we're not certain our straw from sheep and chicken bedding is safe: We only use it on walkways and paths that are downslope of our garden beds. I leave the straw there for two to three years until any residual herbicide has dissipated and broken down into compost, at which point we can scoop it on top of our beds.

At the farm, I do this only because our sheep go through a lot of bedding, and I can't produce enough onsite, so I supplement by buying straw. This leaves us with a lot of bedding to dispose of, and I've found this to be the best way to deal with it in a regenerative way that still has soil benefits. Alternatively, you could pile it and compost it until some radish seeds germinated in the straw compost grow successfully with no indications of herbicide contamination.

Only use straw as mulch if your supplier can guarantee that it hasn't been contaminated with persistent herbicides.

Pine Shavings

If you keep chickens or bunnies, you may be familiar with the pine shavings typically used for their bedding. Because it is finely shredded, this product breaks down quickly, making it an excellent and inexpensive mulch, easy to spread in early spring around annual plants. It is lightweight and easily available, but because it typically needs to be purchased (usually in a plastic bag), we don't buy it specifically for use as mulch. We do gather the used the pine shavings (with dry chicken manure included) from cleaning out our chicken coop and spread it in walkways, just as we do with straw bedding, or add it to our compost pile to contribute nitrogen and kick-start the composting process.

Best for: Mulching around annuals to retain moisture and reduce weed seed germination. The shavings form a dense mat, which is great for plants that prefer moist soil.

Wool

After I saw the results of using wool in my seed-starting mix, I wanted to experiment with other ways to use wool in the garden. A visit to the Stone Barns Center for Food and Agriculture in upstate New York led to an exciting discovery: They were experimenting with wool as a mulch. While it was only being used in a few small spots, they indicated it was working well. I had an excess of raw wool from our sheep and decided to give it a try, first applying it around our cool-season plants such as snap peas. I loved the results. The wool mulch slowly released nitrogen into the soil, it lasted all season, the soil underneath held its moisture well, and the soil temperatures underneath the mulch were regulated perfectly (think of putting a wool sweater over your soil)! While I still don't have enough wool to mulch my entire growing space, I do use as much of it as I can, especially around plants

Pine shavings are lightweight like straw but form a dense mat, which is ideal for plants that prefer moist soil. Here it is used as mulch around a squash seedling.

Mulching the base of a snap pea plant with wool keeps the soil cool and moist, and the wool slowly releases nitrogen into the soil.

that like regular moisture. The wool also serves as a slug repellant, so if your plants are prone to nibbling by those little crawlies, the wool mulch can work well to ward them off.

That said, raw wool can be tough to source. Unless you have your own sheep or know a sheep farmer, it can be difficult and cost prohibitive to acquire, but companies are now popping up to provide wool to gardeners.

Best for: Plants that like moist, cool soils or that are heavy feeders, and plants that are subject to slug damage.

Pebbles

When growing native plants in perennial areas, small rocks and pebbles (called squeegee) are often recommended in dry or semiarid areas because they can mimic the natural landscape. Rocks are often believed to be bad for the soil because they trap excess heat, but in xeriscaped areas with low annual rainfall, native plants and perennials can benefit from a rock mulch rather than wood chip mulch.

Pebbles used for mulch should include smaller rocks less than 1 inch in diameter. Gravel mulch can suppress weed growth and reduce water evaporation. Surprisingly, a rock mulch can also keep the soil below cooler than surfaces mulched with wood chips, and it helps with water infiltration because the rocks don't absorb overhead water or rainfall as wood chips or other mulches do, letting it pass through to the soil. Even a thin layer of gravel can double the amount of moisture that reaches the soil. The downside of using rocks as mulch is, of course, the weight and the inability of rock mulch to add organic matter to the soil.

Best for: Native plantings in more arid climates with rocky soils, and perennial plants that prefer dry, hot climates.

This newer bed is located in a spot with sandy soil. The phosphorus levels are not as high here and the soil is still lacking in some organic matter, so I'm mulching with compost around a cover crop of oats and peas.

Compost

Many gardeners use compost as mulch. Compost can make an excellent mulch, but it needs to be applied thickly (at least 1 to 2 inches thick) to serve as a weed suppressant. Compost also breaks down very quickly, doesn't cool the soil surface as effectively as other mulches, and can create excessively high levels of phosphorus and salinity in soil when applied annually. If using compost as a mulch, be sure to test soil regularly to ensure that salt and nutrient levels aren't getting too high or creating imbalances.

Best for: Mulching around annuals or perennials where soil phosphorous levels are not high.

Grass Clippings

Grass clippings are readily available, which makes them an easy and accessible mulch for many—with a couple of caveats. As with straw, grass clippings may contain herbicides that can leach into your garden soil, so it's essential to use untreated grass clippings. It's also best to avoid grass clippings with weeds that have gone to seed, which will spread to your garden. Grass that has formed seeds can lead to sprouts in your garden soil, but cutting frequently will keep grass from going to seed and provide a good source of free garden mulch. Absolutely avoid using rhizome grasses such as Bermuda or johnsongrass for this purpose, as they can spread by both seed and rhizome.

Apply grass clippings in thin layers, letting one layer dry out before applying the next. Add slowly rather than piling several inches of wet grass all at once, which can form a thick mat that will prevent oxygen and water from reaching the soil and can lead to fungus issues.

Best for: Mulching around annual plants to improve moisture retention and minimize weed seed germination.

Living Mulch

Living mulch, which is sometimes called undercropping, is one way to incorporate more biodiversity into your garden. When using living mulch, we plant into the bare soil around the base of plants to provide soil cover that simultaneously feeds the soil food web.

The downside to this method is that if the living mulch gets too thick, it can outcompete your garden plants for water and nutrients. While it can be tricky to reach the right balance of having enough plants to "mulch" the soil without the plantings becoming *too* thick, it can work in certain circumstances. I've used buckwheat as a living mulch successfully underneath my dahlias. I wait to plant the buckwheat until the dahlias are about a foot tall to ensure the buckwheat won't outcompete the dahlias and overtake them in height. Once the buckwheat blooms, it attracts lots of beneficial insects that help protect my dahlia flowers from pest damage. Before the buckwheat sets seed, I manually crimp it down, and the broken stems dry out and serve as a mulch for the rest of the season.

Buckwheat and nasturtiums form a living mulch under dahlias.

In addition to wood chip mulch, creeping phlox makes a living mulch under peonies.

These onions are underplanted with strawberries for a delicious living mulch. The onions also help deter pests from eating the strawberries.

Sweet potato vines grow along the ground forming a living mulch beneath hydrangeas, providing shade and regulating the soil temperature, which is good for microbial life.

Living mulch can sometimes be as simple as interplanting into a ground-cover crop. For example, I often plant my onions into my strawberry beds. The strawberries provide a good ground cover between the onion bulbs, and the onions help deter nibblers from the strawberries. Where we once had landscape fabric around our peonies, we've planted creeping phlox to help keep the ground cool and provide living cover. It also helps stabilize soils: In some of our unirrigated garden areas where the soil can become quite dry and subject to erosion, we've planted drought-tolerant creeping sedum to help hold soils in place without stealing water from neighboring plants.

Best for: Mulching around tall plants or plants that don't mind some competition. When in doubt, experiment on a small scale and be sure to avoid potentially invasive plants like creeping veronica or microclover, which can become bullies in garden beds.

I terminated this buckwheat by hand at the flowering stage underneath a planting of dahlias.

Terminated Cover Crop

Hands down, my favorite mulch is a terminated cover crop—that is, a cover crop that has been killed back. After all, it's serving multiple purposes: protecting the soil and feeding the soil food web, adding organic matter to deeper layers of soil, and breaking up potential compaction. Typically, we plant cover crops in late summer, let them grow through fall, and select options that winter-kill in our zone. In spring, we are left with the debris from the cover crop, which we simply move aside to create a spot to plant into.

Using a cover crop helps aerate our soil, adds nutrients directly to the root zone, keeps living roots in the soil longer than we typically would have, and blankets the soil over winter—and it's affordable. Cover crop seed is very inexpensive; for our blend that we purchase and mix in bulk, costs are typically around \$5 per 4 × 8-foot bed. Planting a cover crop saves me the expense and labor of amending the soil, meaning it's already in place at planting time so I don't have to transport and apply mulch, and it sustains the soil food web in periods when the beds would otherwise be empty.

Best for: Most purposes. Can be difficult to implement around perennials.

Terminated cover crop is my top choice for mulch in the regenerative garden, but if we don't get a chance to plant a cover crop, I'll go for any of the previously mentioned options that are available (with the exception of compost, as my garden soil is high in phosphorus).

Remember, I use the mulches that are the most readily available to me and that are inexpensive and organic-matter based. If you find another mulch that meets those criteria, go ahead and experiment with it! Coconut husks, wool cuttings, pine boughs, and more can serve as excellent mulches.

After a fall frost, the cover crop of oats has terminated; the peas will die when the temperatures grow colder.

Zinnia seedlings emerge from a spring-terminated cover crop of hairy vetch, which forms a wonderful mulch layer.

When to Mulch

We know that mulch is important to feeding the soil food web and creating a healthy and temperate environment for soil life and plant roots. But is it always wise to use mulch?

There are situations in which we would not want to use certain mulches or where it may even be beneficial to remove mulch from the garden. For example, while mulch will help protect soil from extreme temperature swings over winter, in spring, a very thick layer of leaves or other mulch will keep the soil temperatures lower for longer. This can mean that your soil temperatures may still be too cold for planting when your plants are ready to go.

When a warmer temperature is needed (say, in beds where I will be planting tomatoes, which need a soil temperature of around 60°F/15°C at planting time), clearing away the mulch from the bed a week or two before planting lets the sun's rays warm the soil. We do the same with sweet peas or snap peas, which are planted directly in the ground very early in the season (as early as six weeks before the last frost). That early, the ground could still be frozen at planting depths if the beds remained covered with the winter mulch layer. After planting and after soil temperatures have warmed, the mulch can be replaced.

I generally mulch all of my garden beds for protection over winter, move it aside temporarily in late spring prior to planting to allow the soil to warm, and then slide it back on again once summer temperatures rise to help with moisture retention and weed prevention.

Burlap can be a helpful tool with mulching, especially if using a lightweight mulch like leaves. A layer of burlap placed over the leaves and weighed down with stones or other heavy items will help hold the mulch in place. Burlap can also protect a cover crop from voracious birds in spring and help hold soil temperatures and moisture constant during germination.

Burlap is used to weigh down leaves and prevent them from blowing away over the winter.

I also placed burlap over this bed to protect a cover crop from being eaten by birds.

I battled with a carpet of bindweed that climbed the corn in the background the first year at the farm.

Weed Management for the Regenerative Garden

Dealing with weeds can be one of the most aggravating and time-consuming aspects of gardening. Nothing is more frustrating than going out to relax in the garden and being overwhelmed by rapidly encroaching undesirable plants.

Our first year at the farm, I was absolutely and completely overwhelmed with weeds. Almost the entire 2 acres had some kind of invasive in every square foot: Canada thistle, bindweed, whitetop, bush honeysuckle, Siberian elm, spurge, creeping bellflower. And in addition, I had had a baby in January, so when the weeds started coming in, my youngest was about four months old and my oldest was a toddler (and any parent knows how exhausting that stage is!).

I was burned out that first spring trying to stay on top of it; the weed seed bank at the property is astronomical. To this day, when I hear people say that "a weed is just an unwanted plant," I wince a bit. While this statement can be true, that mindset can also allow for the spread of invasive plants that displace our struggling native habitats, especially in unmanaged natural and riparian areas.

This thicket of thistles on the farm was removed by hand after rains softened the soil sufficiently.

Bindweed will grow through most mulches and is one of the more difficult weeds to manage.

I mulch around our peonies with wood chips to help keep aggressive weeds at bay. The mulch needs refreshing every couple of years or so, depending on how thickly it is applied.

Prioritize Aggressive Spreaders

Do I remove every weed from every square foot of my garden? Absolutely not—I would lose my mind! Instead, I've learned to prioritize one or two weeds each year and focus on trying to eliminate those first. Selecting the most aggressive spreaders and seeders cuts down exponentially on the garden workload each year. The mulch system we rely on helps keep down the rest of the weeds in the meantime.

Proper identification is absolutely key to the weed battle in the garden. Learn about the weeds you see around your space the most. Arm yourself with accurate information so you can be as efficient as possible. This is particularly helpful in early spring. Once you can identify your most frequent weed offenders as tiny sprouts, you will be able to get on top of them before they mature and become difficult and problematic.

For example, once I learned that the whitetop growing on our property was a noxious weed and I was required by our state to eradicate it, I strategized and effectively removed it with occultation. I know exactly what it looks like from first leaves and can spot them from 15 feet away in early spring! If we had waited to eradicate it and planted the perennials that are now in the area where we had the whitetop, occultation would have been out of the question unless we had been willing to also kill newly planted perennials alongside it or use an herbicide.

If the weeds have already gotten away from you or are too difficult to pull, it is best to at least deadhead them before they go to seed. This will keep them from blowing seeds around your beds and creating problems for next season's garden. A moment of time deadheading will save you hours the following spring. Discard any invasive weeds (seeds, plant, or roots) instead of putting them in your compost pile so you don't risk spreading them.

Now that our farm is in its sixth production season, weeds are much less of a problem and are significantly more manageable, thanks to a combination of the following practices.

Do Herbicides Have Any Place in the Regenerative Garden?

The topic of herbicide use is complicated and emotional. After volunteering with local ecological restoration groups, doing a lot of reading on the topic, and engaging in discussions with Dr. Doug Tallamy (an author and leading expert in habitat restoration), we have accepted that judicious herbicide use is sometimes necessary and best for the garden ecosystem, but that the use should be severely limited and only for very specific circumstances.

When to Use Herbicides

The only time we ever use an herbicide in the garden is to paint it by hand onto the cut stumps of particularly aggressive invasive trees and plants, such as common buckthorn, tree of heaven, and bush honeysuckle. Initially, I was strongly opposed to herbicide use on our property. For three years, I cut down sprouts and suckers of these plants, which had been allowed to grow unchecked for decades. And I began noticing something: The invasive shrubs and trees that I pulled or cut would come back stronger and bushier every year. This is part of why invasive plants are so damaging to ecosystems. They spread rapidly, and a pruning is usually encouragement for them to grow even faster. Simultaneously, they can change the actual chemistry of the soil food web in their rhizosphere to be less hospitable for native plants and make their own survival more likely.

After reading Dr. Tallamy's book *Nature's Best Hope*, I decided to try his method of brushing a systemic herbicide onto the stump of the invasive plant immediately after cutting. This allows the herbicide to work its way into the vigorous root of the invasive and kill it from where it grows. Finally, we made progress on the Siberian elm suckers, common buckthorn, Japanese knotweed, and honeysuckles in our woods. As we did, the native American plum trees, chokecherries, and currants began to thrive. Finally, I could seed the area with blue grama without it being outcompeted by invasive plant suckers. It was incredible to see, after two years of stubbornness, how quickly it worked—and we never once had to spray anything on our soil.

A Last Resort

This is not to say that I recommend this practice for all weeds. Far from it—it should be used only as a last resort and in the case of invasive plants that cannot be pulled or otherwise manually removed. Consult with your state extension service first to determine whether mechanical control is possible for invasive weeds. It is important to understand how vital the battle against invasive plants is, given our current global climate; we will discuss that more in the chapter on plant selection.

Types of Weeds

There are many ways to control weeds, and the strategies you choose will depend on the weed itself, its growth habits, and its level of invasiveness, if any. When I think about weed removal, I categorize those plants into two groups.

Rhizome-based. These spread underground via a root system. An example is bindweed: Its roots are notoriously deep growing (some have been recorded reaching depths of around 15 feet!) and pernicious, resprouting and growing rapidly from various points along that rhizome. It is important to know whether a weed is rhizome-based. If it is, you'll want to avoid soil disturbance methods such as tillage at all costs, which will just serve to chop up that rhizome into hundreds of pieces from which it can propagate. Similarly, gardeners will want to avoid composting any part of a rhizome-based weed, as it can form roots and resprout easily from cuttings and fragments of the plant.

Taproot. These weeds, including burdock, mallow, dandelion, and pigweed amaranth, grow a large taproot underground and embed themselves deep into soil. They are quite common in compacted soils, where they can actually be somewhat beneficial, because those deep taproots extract nutrients and minerals and bring them to the surface through the plants' leaves, which can then break down on the surface of the soil. Because of this, many gardeners even claim that taproot weeds such as dandelions can "heal" the soil. This may be true, but it would take a very long time, and in the meantime your dandelions will drive you and your neighbors crazy (and could outcompete important native plants).

Invasive smooth brome, common on our property, must be carefully pulled when soil is wet to get its long, spreading rhizomes.

The taproots of a young mallow weed (left) and Queen Anne's lace (right) extend deep into the soil.

I add a thick layer of leaves between the rosebushes. Although the leaves would blow away in a less-protected area of the garden, the roses help hold them in place.

Applying a thick layer of wood chips is one way to prepare a previously weedy area for a new planting. The wood chips smother the weeds while enriching the soil.

Weed Management Strategies

The key with all weeds is to stay on top of removing them in spring or early summer while they are small, before they've had a chance to establish and go to seed. Here are several methods.

Deep mulches. Earlier in this chapter, we discussed the benefits of using mulches. They are not only good for maintaining soil health, temperature, and moisture, but they are key to reducing weed density. Use thick layers of mulch for best results. If desired seedlings are still small and at risk of being swallowed by mulch, be sure to clear the mulch back a few inches from plants.

Manual removal. With the exception of rhizome-based weeds, small weed sprouts can simply be pulled from the soil and left on the surface to compost. Gardens benefit from this breakdown of organic matter, which will happen very quickly when weeds are still small. Be sure to remove weeds before they have gone to seed! This is where weed identification again becomes important, as some weeds form seeds that are very difficult to see while the plants are quite young, and in those cases you may inadvertently spread them on your garden soil when the weeds are left on the surface. When in doubt, use the weeds to create a weed tea (see page 185), which will make weed seeds no longer viable. Rhizome-based weeds are trickier because they grow belowground and often produce seeds as well. They may require more aggressive removal methods. Contact your state extension service for help identifying best practices for each weed variety.

Occultation, done by laying a black tarp over a bed, can eliminate existing weeds and reduce the germination rate of the surface s eed bank as well. Unfortunately, it will not work well for rhizome-based weeds.

Occultation. We've already explored occultation with black plastic as a means of preparing a lawn or yard space for a garden; it is a viable method for eliminating weeds and for reducing the germination rates of the surface weed seed bank as well. I prefer to use occultation only for large areas where hand-pulling is not an option, due to the method's impact on surface soil life and the amount of plastic needed to complete it. Occultation may not work for all weeds; for example, rhizome-based weeds with deep roots, such as bindweed, will not be killed all the way down and will likely regrow.

Crowding. Crowding plants is one of the most effective means of reducing weed pressure at the farm. Not only have I found that most of our plants can be spaced more closely than recommended, allowing for higher production, but as the plants grow and block sunlight from the surface of the soil, fewer weeds germinate. Yes, some weeds do manage to poke through (especially when the plants are still young and small), but crowding and dense planting have led to great success in our battle against weeds without requiring much additional time to implement. There is always a risk of plants competing against each other too much, leading to stunted growth, so be mindful not to place plants too close. It can help to put less deeply rooted plants, such as thyme and other shallow herbs, next to deeper-rooted plants like tomatoes to help minimize competition. Similarly, shorter plants can be used to crowd out potential weeds next to taller plants.

What About Pre-emergents?

Pre-emergents are chemicals applied to the soil before weed seeds germinate and emerge from the ground. These herbicides work by creating a barrier in the soil that prevents weed seeds from sprouting or inhibits their root growth, thus helping control weeds before they establish. I often see pre-emergents recommended as an alternative to herbicide use; however, these chemicals should not be used in the regenerative garden. Not only do pre-emergents have massive detrimental impacts on aquatic life (and yes, all of our garden inputs eventually make it into the water table, even if you aren t near a waterway), they are relatively unstudied. Their impact on pollinators and the soil food web is largely unknown.

Crowding plants is an alternative to mulching and reduces weed pressure.

5

Plant for Ecosystem Health

EVERY CHOICE WE MAKE within our garden ripples through the web of biodiversity, impacting not only the immediate environment but the broader ecosystem as well. Each plant, whether native or introduced, carries the potential to either enrich or disrupt the delicate balance. Invasive species, for example, pose threats to local flora and fauna and compromise the resiliency of ecosystems, including that of the soil food web. Through careful consideration and conscious decision-making, we embark on a journey toward cultivating gardens that not only thrive in harmony with nature but also serve as sanctuaries for biodiversity conservation.

A young and hungry grasshopper climbs a stem.

Planting for biodiversity increases garden resilience. The tomato plant is less tempting to pests when underplanted with a trap crop such as nasturtium; lavender attracts pollinators; and nearby native virgin's bower attracts beneficials.

Plant for Biodiversity

Planting for biodiversity means growing a wide range of plants that support a diverse and healthy ecosystem, and it typically results in gardens that are the most resilient and easiest to care for. By planting a wide variety of plants and spreading them throughout the garden, you will find that the garden's resistance to pests and disease is greatly improved. When pests do arrive in your garden, they'll be much less likely to spread if you have a varied collection of plants in one space.

Interplanting to Reduce Pest Damage

Diversifying your garden beds by interplanting can give plants a leg up against pest damage.

Limit the buffet. Gardeners are often encouraged to kill the destructive tomato hornworm, for example, because it eats large amounts of plant matter in a short period of time and therefore can be very destructive to tomato and pepper plants. But the tomato hornworm metamorphoses into a native pollinator moth that is actually important to the garden ecosystem, so killing it is not ideal.

To limit the damage the hornworm can cause, avoid providing it with a buffet: Instead of planting all of your tomatoes in one bed, spread them out in the garden, and interplant them with other plant species native to your area to attract parasitic wasps that feed on and use the tomato hornworm as a host.

Relocation is another great alternative to killing hornworms (or losing your tomato plants). I typically have a couple of sacrificial tomato plants growing somewhere in the garden, and I can relocate a tomato hornworm onto one as a host plant if it decides to make our garden a home during its caterpillar stage.

Powdery mildew and fungi. Powdery mildew and other common fungi that attack specific plants are much less likely to spread if you have diversified garden beds. If you've ever had powdery mildew in your garden, you know that it can spread quickly, especially to other susceptible plants.

When we started our farm, I thought planting pumpkins next to our peonies was a good idea, but it turns out that both plants are susceptible

Strawberries, scented geranium, and peppers are interplanted with a native goldenrod to create visual appeal while reducing the potential for widespread pest damage due to both native plants and biodiversity of plantings.

to powdery mildew. In hindsight, placing those two plants adjacent to one another contributed to the rapid proliferation of the fungus through my farm. Now I'm careful to plant cucumbers, squash, and other susceptible crops next to resistant plants, such as geraniums, rather than next to susceptible plants like zinnia or bee balm.

There are so many guides out there detailing what plants like to coexist and warning about which plants to avoid placing near others—it's impossible to follow them all! Rather, pay attention to what pests and diseases affect your garden most frequently, and plan your garden accordingly.

Native Plants Support Wildlife

Native plants are a major piece of biodiversity often missing in most home gardens, resulting in a gap in the native insects and animals they support. Native plants weren't always a focus here in my garden. They were the last thing on my mind when we started the farm. While in those days I knew that we had voracious and aggressive weeds, I didn't understand the severity or how desperately our land was crying out for native plants and habitat.

Native Plants to Attract Birds

The first year at the farm, I was in survival mode, trying to keep the bindweed from pulling down every single cornstalk and zinnia we grew and fighting late (and early) frosts and hailstorms. We had ravenous pests that first year: I would come out in the morning to skeletonized leaves and shreds of petals hanging on to dahlias. I began creeping out at night, headlamp on like some sort of midnight grave robber, to investigate, finding swarms of earwigs covering our plants so thickly that individual plants weren't visible through the tangle of legs and antennae.

It had been a terrible growing year anyway, so I didn't do much to mitigate the earwigs other than set out some traps (soy sauce and a splash of vegetable oil in tuna cans) and cover unopened dahlia blooms with organza bags so I'd have something left to harvest. But over winter, I had time to pause and think critically about what we were seeing in the garden.

A robin perches on the fence, watching carefully for caterpillars to feed its young hatchlings nearby in this pocket meadow of native plants adjacent to a vegetable garden.

SUPPORT INSECT LIFE TO SUPPORT BIRD LIFE

As I researched, the most recommended solution to earwigs was to scatter a mix of boric acid and diatomaceous earth (DE) along the ground. But a little more research revealed that DE would not only kill earwigs, it would also kill spiders, ground-dwelling bees, and basically any soft-bodied insect that came across the powder. I knew from sitting and examining my garden with my toddler that insects were everywhere along the soil level. Was it reasonable to expect that no bugs other than the target earwigs would meander across the DE? Of course not—many other beings, beneficials included, would be negatively impacted by this application.

Instead, I turned to one of the natural predators of the earwig: birds. After decades of neglect and invasive plants, our garden wasn't exactly inviting to our feathered friends. I knew that we had chokecherries in our woods, a native shrub that serves as an excellent plant for bird habitat and provides small berries that are a favorite bird food. The chokecherries were few and far between, outcompeted by towering invasive Siberian elms and common buckthorns, so we decided our first effort to fix our earwig problem would be to rehabilitate the chokecherries and add more plants that would naturally attract avian friends. As we cut back those invasive plants, sweating and stabbed by thorns while chipping away tons of dead and twisted wood, I wondered if it would be worth it.

One day the following spring, I took a load of compost to the woods and caught a whiff of the most incredible fragrance: It was the chokecherries and American plums blooming, thriving with the sunlight we had provided by whacking back the surrounding invasive plants. As spring wore on, birds arrived to nest in the understory habitat provided by the shrubs, and their chirping as they flitted around the berries filled the hot summer air. They perched on the branches of the currants, occasionally swooping down to a dahlia head to snap up an earwig.

A flock of birds flies over the main garden to rest in the chokecherry thicket adjacent to the space. They are attracted by the native plants and, in staying, help balance the ecosystem of the garden.

Were the earwigs nonexistent in year two? No, but they were significantly reduced compared to the previous year. So we added 30 native golden currant plants to the field, and three years later, we miraculously no longer needed to bag our dahlias to protect them from earwigs. Birds are constantly hopping around the currant rows, rifling through the soil mulch for buggy snacks.

No Such Thing as "Pest-Free"

Incorporating native plants isn't a magic bullet to pest prevention. But once you understand why a pest-free garden is unrealistic, you can also recognize that not having any pests would be terrible for the ecosystem. Do we really want to eliminate *all* of the caterpillars that nibble on the leaves, killing the main food source for baby birds? Do we want *all* aphids eradicated, meaning we'd never get to see ladybugs, which eat the aphids, again in the garden?

It will take time for nature to balance our garden ecosystem. Meanwhile, physical barriers help: Drawstring organza bags placed over vulnerable blooms (like dahlias) can prevent grasshoppers, earwigs, and Japanese beetles from attacking them while we work toward ecosystem balance in the garden. Draping insect netting over young squash plants can block squash vine borers without using damaging pesticides. Physical barriers help minimize frustration as well as the urge to employ pesticides.

A focus on eliminating all pests won't work; that's just not how nature functions. But a focus on boosting the ecosystem and reducing opportunities for pests to do major plant damage will do wonders!

Plant Native Plants to Attract Beneficial Insects

Having a diverse range of native plants assists the garden by attracting a range of beneficial insects and parasitic wasps. While nonnative plants are capable of attracting beneficials, albeit to a lesser extent, native plants excel at it. But look up "beneficial plants" for interplanting in the garden, and you'll get a laundry list of nonnatives (and even invasives): dill, fennel, nasturtium, sweet alyssum. While yes, these nonnatives can be part of any good biodiversity planting in the garden, native beneficial plants have coevolved over millions of years alongside the native beneficial insects that thrive in and support our garden climates and ecosystems. In some cases, insects—like the monarchs, which require milkweed to survive—will only eat or reproduce on specific native plants.

Native plants differ by location and ecoregion. For best results, seek out plants that are specifically native to your state or a neighboring state with a similar climate. (When discussing native plants, we typically don't differentiate by USDA Hardiness Zones, which are based on temperature ranges, not regional characteristics.)

Rudbeckia triloba, *blue grama, agastache, and sunflowers in the foreground with switchgrasses and native prairie behind provide a healthy buffet for beneficial insects to guard the vegetable garden and nearby greenhouse.*

Native Plants and the Good Bugs They Attract

Even when you ensure biodiversity and interplant with natives specifically meant to attract beneficials, it is highly likely that your garden will experience pest damage from time to time. Try not to step in and interfere with this process, difficult as it may be to see your prized roses and favorite tomato plant nibbled.

Fascinating research in the field of entomology tells us that as plants are attacked by pests, they send out distress signals designed to attract beneficials. As a corn plant is gnawed on by a corn earworm, for example, the plant responds by releasing blends of 10 to 12 volatile chemical compounds that communicate the identity of their attacker to the beneficial parasitic wasps that favor those pests. Not only does this reduce pest pressure on the plant, it aids the survival of the parasitic wasp: By releasing this plume of compounds into the air, the plant helps the wasps quickly and efficiently find the attacker.

Interfering with this signaling process—even by removing pest-damaged leaves—can stop this valuable interaction from occurring between plant and beneficial insect. Even worse, if we spray our plants with pesticide, we risk inadvertently killing the beneficials that arrive to eat the pests.

Parasitic wasps, for example, use specific caterpillars as hosts, laying eggs within the caterpillar body. As the wasp larvae hatch, they consume the host from the inside out before emerging (horrifying, yes). These wasps offer your garden protection against excessive numbers of nibbling caterpillars, keeping the balance in check. However, let's say a gardener sees caterpillars attacking and sprays with neem oil, thinking that it is a safe option for the garden ecosystem. The unintended consequences can be wide ranging. Not only will it kill the caterpillars feeding on the sprayed plant, it will also suffocate any parasitic wasps or soft-bodied beneficials (which can be very small and difficult to see when hiding in blooms and under leaves) as well as pollinators like bees that come in contact with the neem oil. A parasitic wasp may have already shown up on the scene to assist and lay eggs in the caterpillar host, but if you spray, all of these potential garden defenders will die alongside the pest.

It can be difficult and frustrating to hand the control over to nature in the short term, but in the long term, providing the right conditions to support the ecosystem will result in a healthier and more well-balanced garden without the need for additional effort and inputs from the gardener.

Establishing the right conditions involves interplanting, providing biodiversity, avoiding monocultures in the garden, and even including trap crops when necessary. The following pages will discuss how to create biodiversity in the garden in a bit more detail.

Hoverflies are valuable beneficial insects, devouring aphids and contributing to healthy ecosystems.

A dragonfly carcass found in the garden. Dragonflies help reduce mosquito populations.

North American Native Plants for Attracting Beneficial Insects

Common Name(s)	Botanical Name	Soil Preference	Beneficials Attracted	Annual or Perennial	USDA Hardiness Zones	Notes
Annual buckwheat	*Eriogonum annuum*	Dry	Big-eyed bugs, damsel bugs, lacewings, ladybugs, minute pirate bugs, parasitic wasps, tachinid flies, and more	Mostly annual	Varies	Can be an aggressive self-seeder
Aster	*Symphyotrichum* species	Varied	Damsel bugs, ladybugs, minute pirate bugs, parasitic wasps, soldier beetles, tachinid flies	Perennial	3–8	Late, delicate flowers
Common boneset	*Eupatorium perfoliatum*	Damp	Damsel bugs, ladybugs, minute pirate bugs, parasitic wasps, tachinid flies	Perennial	3–8	Tolerant of sun and shade; best if purchased as plants
Common sunflower	*Helianthus annuus*	Dry	Assassin bugs, big-eyed bugs, lacewings, minute pirate bugs, predatory stink bugs, robber flies, soldier beetles, spiders, and more	Annual	n/a	Can reseed prolifically; good for attracting birds
Common yarrow	*Achillea millefolium*	Dry	Damsel bugs, lacewings, ladybugs, parasitic wasps, syrphid flies	Perennial	3–8	Spreads readily
Coreopsis, tickseed	*Coreopsis* species	Dry	Lacewings, minute pirate bugs, parasitic wasps, soldier beetles, spiders	Short-lived perennial	3–8	Long flowering period
Coyote brush	*Baccharis pilularis*	Dry	Lacewings, ladybugs, minute pirate bugs, parasitic wasps, syrphid flies	Perennial	Species dependent	Good for hedgerows (evergreen shrub)
Culver's root	*Veronicastrum virginicum*	Average–wet	Minute pirate bugs, native bees, parasitic wasps, syrphid flies	Perennial	3–8	Small white spike flowers
Cup plant, compass plant	*Silphium perfoliatum*	Dry	Lacewings, ladybugs, minute pirate bugs, soldier bugs, spiders	Perennial	3–9	Very tall, spreader; may take over smaller gardens
False aster	*Boltonia asteroides*	Dry	Big-eyed bugs, ladybugs, minute pirate bugs, tachinid flies, soldier beetles, syrphid flies	Perennial	4–9	Many cultivars available
Golden alexanders	*Zizia aurea*	Average–wet	Parasitic flies, parasitic wasps, soldier beetles, and countless others	Perennial	4–9	Yellow umbel flowers
Goldenrod	*Solidago* species	Average–moist	Assassin bugs, big-eyed bugs, damsel bugs, ladybugs, minute pirate bugs, parasitic wasps, soldier beetles, spiders, syrphid flies, and others	Perennial	4–9	Beautiful blooms in late summer/early fall

Common Name(s)	Botanical Name	Soil Preference	Beneficials Attracted	Annual or Perennial	USDA Hardiness Zones	Notes
Heart-leaved meadow parsnip, heartleaf alexanders	*Zizia aptera*	Dry–average	Countless beneficials	Perennial	4–9	A dryland version of golden alexander with yellow umbel flowers
Hoary vervain	*Verbena stricta*	Average	Damsel bugs, lacewings, minute pirate bugs, parasitic wasps, spiders	Short-lived perennial	3–7	Easy to start from seed
Lacy phacelia, fiddleneck	*Phacelia tanacetifolia*	Dry–average	Parasitic wasps (some), syrphid flies, tachinid flies	Annual	n/a	Long blooming; can be used as cover crop
Low calamint	*Clinopodium arkansanum*	Medium	Countless beneficials	Perennial	4–8	Tolerates shallow/rocky soils
Meadowsweet	*Spiraea alba*	Average–wet	Assassin bugs, damsel bugs, ground beetles, ladybugs, minute pirate bugs, parasitic wasps, and others	Perennial	4–9	Deciduous shrub; beautiful white blooms for pollinators
Mountain mint	*Pycnanthemum* species	Average–moist	Countless beneficials	Perennial	3–9	Spreads, but not aggressive like common mint
Pinnate prairie coneflower, gray-headed coneflower	*Ratibida pinnata*	Average	Damsel bugs, lacewings, ladybugs, minute pirate bugs, parasitic wasps, soldier beetles, spiders, syrphid flies, tachinid flies	Perennial	3–9	Prefers lean soil
Rudbeckia	*Rudbeckia* species	Dry–average	Parasitic wasps (some), soldier beetles, syrphid flies, tachinid flies	Depends on variety	Depends on variety	Great cut flowers
Shrubby cinquefoil	*Dasiphora fruticosa* ssp. *floribunda*	Varied	Lacewings, ladybugs, minute pirate bugs, parasitic wasps, syrphid flies	Perennial	2–7	Evergreen shrub
Smooth oxeye	*Heliopsis helianthoides*	Varied	Ladybugs, lacewings, parasitic wasps, soldier beetles, syrphid flies, tachinid flies	Perennial	3–9	Prone to aphid attacks, which in turn attract those insects that eat aphids
Spotted bee balm, horsemint	*Monarda punctata*	Dry	Countless beneficials	Perennial	4–9	Deer resistant, stunning flower

Dahlias are underplanted with buckwheat and nasturtium (which also functions as a trap crop). It's important to wait to plant the buckwheat until the dahlias are established so it doesn't overtake them.

Practical Ways to Increase Biodiversity

While it can be easy to get bogged down in detailed guides that tell gardeners, "Plant X next to Y, but don't plant X next to Z!" the reality is, it can be much simpler than that. Planting a wide range of species together, as well as planting beneficial natives, is an effective way to add biodiversity to and benefit the garden ecosystem.

Companion Planting and Interplanting

Intermixing plant species in the garden mimics nature's entropy. It is not only a horticultural technique but a testament to our symbiotic relationship with the natural world. I try not to get too caught up in the many rules out there about interplanting and instead focus on my garden goals of biodiversity. That said, there are a few important principles to keep in mind.

In our garden, interplantings support biodiversity, including (from left) zinnias with basil, asters with dahlias, rudbeckias with lettuces and beans, and roses with alliums.

Keep in mind plant heights and habits. Avoid placing plants that get too tall and floppy next to walkways where they will droop over and become a nuisance. Place shorter and varying-height plants near path edges, with increasing heights toward the garden bed's center. Similarly, don't place a very large or tall plant to the south of a smaller plant where it will cast too much shade (unless the smaller one is a shade-loving plant!). Shade- or cool-loving plants like lettuces and cilantro can benefit from being slightly shaded by a companion plant; for example, I like to plant a row of lettuces under a tomato trellis in the garden, which naturally provides some shade and keeps the lettuces producing into the hotter summer months.

At the farm, I frequently interplant my dahlias with buckwheat, which is excellent at attracting ladybugs and other beneficials and doesn't compete with the dahlia tuber's roots. I've learned, however, that I have to plant them after the dahlias are established. If I plant them at the same time, the buckwheat grows so quickly that it overtakes the dahlias! This doesn't mean that we can't plant tall plants with shorter plants, but it does mean that we should be mindful of positioning. Place taller plants on the north side of shorter plants so as not to block the sunlight for others.

Balance producer plants and trap crops. Trap crops are sacrificial plants, basically providing pests with a food alternative to the plant you wish to harvest. When we employ a trap crop in coordination with plants meant to attract a good diversity of native beneficial insects, we may see greater success by building the population of beneficial insects over the long term versus employing broad-spectrum pesticides. There are many anecdotal tales of trap crops being effective in garden applications, but there are as many anecdotes about them *not* working and a lack of scientific evidence as to their effectiveness.

The tall trellis covered with pumpkins in this photo is located north of the garden to prevent them from shading out the sun-loving foreground plants as they climb. Meanwhile, plants that appreciate cooler temperatures in summer, such as clematis, lettuces, and cilantro, enjoy the shade created by the trellis.

If you grow vegetables, be sure to incorporate equal amounts of producer plants (tomatoes, cucumbers, lettuce, etc.) with herbs, trap crops, and plants that serve and attract beneficial insects, rotating plant type every couple of feet.

For example, I plant our squash, tomatoes, nasturtium, echinacea, and lavender in an area adjacent to an American plum shrub. The native plum attracts the birds that help keep squash vine borers and other caterpillars at bay, and the flowers attract beneficials.

Not only does planting this way create lots of biodiversity in the garden, it is visually stimulating and helps reduce disease and pest pressures.

While some scientific studies have been done, strong research evidence indicating the effectiveness of frequently recommended companion plantings is lacking. Instead, I like to rely on the simple and easy recommendation to grow as biodiverse a garden as possible, and I keep in mind the following considerations to do so.

Consider low-growing ground covers. Low-growing plants that spread to create living shade for the garden soil increase biodiversity in the garden while providing soil benefits. Living mulches help maintain even soil temperatures and moisture levels, which bolster the function of the microbes and soil food web.

But watch out for invasives. However, many plants that are frequently recommended as living ground covers, such as sweet alyssum, can be invasive in some gardens, so do your research first! Some pretty underplantings we've used as living ground covers include sweet potato vine and petunias. We once tried microclover but found it to spread and creep excessively and create problems in the garden when used as a perennial ground cover.

One of the most frequently recommended trap crops/companion plantings I see is nasturtium to mitigate aphids. However, as a nonnative plant, nasturtium's effectiveness in attracting beneficials and supporting the garden ecosystem is limited, even more so when we consider that nasturtium can be an invasive plant in USDA Zones warmer than 9. The same can be said for the frequently

Pumpkin plants grow among American plums, which attract birds and serve as bird habitat. The proximity of the native plant provides natural bird protection against squash vine borers.

recommended sweet alyssum, which turns into a garden bully in warmer zones and is on the invasives list in coastal California, for one.

This is not to say that nonnative plants can't be beneficial; after all, many of our edible plants are nonnative and can contribute to biodiversity. Nasturtium can still be helpful as a trap crop (we've shown it in this book!), but it should be watched carefully for aggressive spreading and planted with native plants alongside. Regionality is a key consideration here. In my hardiness zone, nasturtium seeds do not survive our colder winters, making it an option, but it's still not as good as a native plant if the goal is attracting beneficials like ladybugs. This is where perimeter plantings of natives such as coreopsis, yarrow, goldenrod, and pearly everlasting can be more beneficial. When in doubt, start with a small patch of nonnatives and evaluate for success and potential invasiveness before planting them on a wide scale in your garden.

Plant a border of native perennials. Native plants can be tricky to include in an annual garden due to their size and spread. Yarrow, for example, can be excellent in a perimeter planting but can quickly take over a raised bed. Using native plants as a border in your more permanent landscaping may be a better way to attract greater numbers of beneficial insects that will naturally help protect your garden. Once you have a stronger understanding of how various native plants perform in your climate and which ones are less aggressive spreaders or smaller in stature, you can experiment with mixing them into your annual garden spaces. Note that if a desired companion plant seems to seed heavily, you can mitigate this by fall deadheading.

Through plantings that emphasize biodiversity in the garden space, we unlock myriad benefits for the garden. Enhancing the diversity of the soil food web begins at the microbial level, and having a variety of plants putting off various root exudates not only helps prevent spread of disease but attracts a greater web of insects (both beneficial and not), which is key to a naturally pest-resistant garden.

The perennial native plantings in the foreground attract beneficial insects that help protect the crops in the annual production beds next to the greenhouse.

Assess soil preference. Plants in the same bed will perform best if they have similar soil needs. For example, don't plant a dry soil–loving plant like sedum next to a plant that enjoys regular water, such as hydrangea. One will end up unhappy! Instead, focus on like with like: plants that prefer moist soils together, and plants that prefer dry soils together.

Allelopathy. *Allelopathy* refers to the tendency of one plant to change soil characteristics to make growing conditions less amenable to other nearby plants so it can access more nutrients. While sunflowers can be beautiful in the garden (and perform phytoremediation in contaminated soils), they have an allelopathic tendency that can make them a poor companion planting option. So as you devise companion planting, research whether your planned garden plants have allelopathic tendencies.

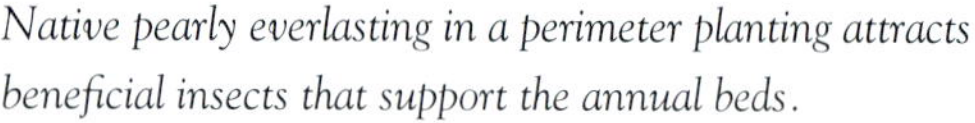

Native pearly everlasting in a perimeter planting attracts beneficial insects that support the annual beds.

Yarrow is a wonderful attractant of tachinid flies. This variety is a cultivar, so it is less likely to spread aggressively, but it still attracts numerous beneficial insects to our farm.

Select Plants Strategically for Your Needs

Thoroughly researching the habits of the plants you plan to use is one of the most important parts of incorporating biodiversity and native plants in the garden. Knowing every plant's growth habits, reseeding patterns, mature size, and potential for underground spread is key when planning for interplanting.

For example, planting yarrow, a native but aggressive spreader, into a raised bed will have you cursing the day you read about the plant; putting it into a perimeter landscape area that doesn't have water access and where nothing else grows will give the plant room to spread without being a nuisance.

And while milkweed is a beautiful and vital plant for our native monarchs (and happens to attract one of the widest ranges of beneficial insects in my garden), it also creates and drops many seeds and spreads rapidly—perhaps not the best option for a vegetable production garden but wonderful for an unused alley or side yard.

NATIVE CULTIVARS FOR SMALLER SPACES

There is hot debate in the native gardening world around the use of native cultivars, with many proponents saying that planting the straight native species (versus a hybridized cultivar) is the only way to go. Others argue that cultivars of native plants can serve as a gateway to appreciating native plants. Commonly sold in garden centers today, cultivars have been bred to have different traits than the native species, such as uprightness, different color blooms, or smaller statures that fit into tighter urban and suburban

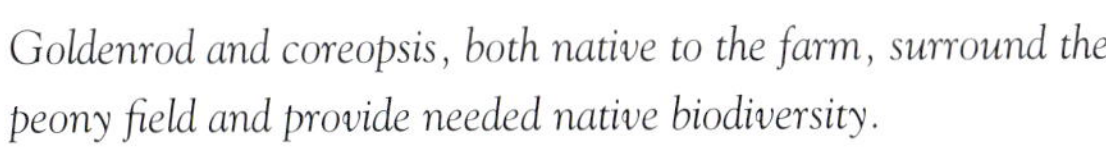

Goldenrod and coreopsis, both native to the farm, surround the peony field and provide needed native biodiversity.

A native variety of echinacea in a landscape area is popular with swallowtail butterflies and other pollinators.

gardens. These traits make more home gardeners inclined to plant them.

I tend to fall somewhere in the middle of the debate. While I agree that the straight native species are always best for attracting and feeding beneficials and pollinators, their tendency to get large and spread can make them unpopular choices in tight spaces, and I would rather encourage someone to plant a native cultivar than a nonnative or even invasive plant. Urban gardeners operating in smaller spaces might benefit from planting native cultivars, which are often smaller than their full-size siblings but with all the same bloom and leaf characteristics of the parent plant. While the science is always evolving, current research indicates that cultivars that remain as similar as possible to the original plant (in bloom color, shape, and leaf color) can still provide ecosystem benefits for native insects and ecosystems.

Many cultivars also tend to be less aggressive as spreaders than the straight native species. Our 'Firefly Peach Sky' yarrow, for example, is often covered with beneficial insects but has not spread beyond its original planting. Contrast this with the white native species, which reseeds happily all over the landscape. The cultivar can be an appealing option for home gardeners who don't want to be fighting reseeding and potentially aggressive native plants but still wish to provide pollinator and ecosystem support.

So don't despair if your garden can't sustain a 7-foot-tall Joe-Pye weed or towering echinacea plant; a cultivar might attract vital native pollinators nearly as well.

This thicket of chokecherry underbrush is only about 15 feet in diameter, but it is always full of bird activity.

A birdbath in the foreground attracts birds to the garden in the background. Native goldenrod in the background provides seeds for winter forage.

Plant for Habitat Creation

We often focus on how plants in the garden can serve us, the gardeners, without considering those plants' significant roles within the greater garden ecosystem—roles that have little to do with our goals for the garden.

Many of our native bird–supporting understory shrubs aren't "pretty" by modern horticulture's standards and don't produce food for us, but these shrubs provide birds with low habitat, food sources, and protected areas to nest within. We tend to glance over them because they often become overgrown and unkempt and don't fit our aesthetic of a landscaped yard—but they are just what birds need to feel safe.

Since incorporating overgrown and unwieldy golden currant hedgerows in our garden, we frequently observe finches and robins divebombing us for snacks as we bend and harvest—and we see significantly fewer nibbling pests. Because we reestablished the habitat that had been missing from our garden ecosystem, nature is able to find balance.

Pay Attention to Spacing

Consider spacing as well as plant habits when planning for garden biodiversity. Native perennial plants often need more space; others, like annuals, can benefit from close planting.

We find that placing annuals tightly supports biodiversity; the close proximity seems to mimic the entropy of nature. Planting diverse annuals in a small space provides ecosystem diversity while minimizing the number of weeds that germinate. For example, the average recommended spacing between tomato plants is 18 to 24 inches. That recommendation could be interpreted to mean nothing should be planted 18 to 24 inches around a tomato, but we prefer to plant low-growing ground covers, such as thyme, around tomato plants, supplementing with native bloomers such as coreopsis or rudbeckia to attract beneficials.

We take care to space perennial plants, expecting spread. Many native perennials grow

The first year, we had lots of space between plants in the pocket meadow.

By the second year, the pocket meadow had started to fill in but was not yet at maturity.

By year three, the pocket meadow (shown here from a different angle) had matured and filled in. Spacing with perennials requires a bit more caution: It can be easy to fill a plot with many plants in year one when they are small, but this ultimately results in overcrowding. It's better to allow space at first and fill in gaps over time, meanwhile mulching in between them.

I often plant my annuals a bit tighter than the recommended spacing to help crowd out potential weeds.

Pumpkins climb a trellis underplanted with buckwheat, which attracts pollinators and other beneficials that help reduce pest damage and increase yield.

slowly for the first two or three years, then explode into growth and quickly spread. Planting these too closely together in year one can ultimately cause them to struggle and compete with one another in the long term. That said, in the first couple of seasons, you can plant annuals tightly around well-spaced larger perennials while the perennials get established. This will not only ensure more biodiversity and weed suppression but will make your garden rich with texture and color. As the garden evolves and expands, dividing plants to help minimize spread is another good option.

Set Realistic Expectations

We have realized along our journey that we simply shouldn't grow certain plants at our farm, at least not with the expectation of ever getting significant harvests from them.

One of these is roses. In our area, Japanese beetles are rampant. This invasive pest lacks many native predators, aside from birds and a parasitic wasp that is just starting to use Japanese beetles as a host—let's keep our fingers crossed on that one! It's very difficult to manage Japanese beetles on roses. (If you've had them, you know—turn your back for one day from the daily routine of handpicking and dropping the beetles into a jar of soapy water, and they've completely destroyed an entire bush of new buds.) Therefore I've simply stopped adding roses to our landscape.

I haven't pulled our existing roses yet, though I've certainly considered it, but I do not expect any harvestable or good-looking roses from July through late August, and I certainly wouldn't make them a focal point of my garden landscaping. Part of gardening with realistic expectations is the ongoing evaluation of the plants selected for the garden and whether they thrive in the climate and soil and with the pest pressure you have.

In our region, Japanese beetles are incredibly aggressive with roses. We've taken to interplanting roses with garlic in an attempt to deter the beetles.

Avoid Invasive Plants

While we've discussed the importance of native plants as a key component of biodiversity success, we must pay equal consideration to what we should *not* include in our gardens. Invasive plants pose a danger to the ecological health of the landscape, and they can throw off the balance of a healthy regenerative garden.

What Are Invasive Plants?

Invasive plants are nonnative plants that spread and reproduce aggressively and rapidly, outcompeting natives, taking over natural areas, and creating monocultures. In the absence of any of their home country's native biological agents or insect controls, they adapt to new areas easily and are defined as harming a region's property, economy, or native plants and animals. As invasive plants move into an area, they typically displace important native plants, causing major problems for indigenous populations of insects, birds, and ecosystems as a whole.

Invasive plants displace the native species needed desperately by specialist insects, bees in particular: Many native bees require specific nectar sources and hosts for reproduction. Squash bees, for example, are specialist pollinators of cucurbits (squash, pumpkins, and cucumbers). Blueberry digger bees are blueberry specialist pollinators. Perhaps the most well-known example of a plant with a specialist insect relationship is milkweed, which has been systematically removed from much of the North American prairies due to its toxicity to grazing cattle and propensity to spread into farmlands. The plant is the only host for the monarch caterpillar; monarchs have evolved to specifically utilize milkweed plants as a larval host and also as nectar for adult butterflies.

Creeping bellflower is a pernicious and aggressive invasive weed at the farm, and we fight it constantly, as it spreads via underground rhizome and is rampant in neighbors' yards.

Resident sheep Roosevelt helps eat down some of the invasive smooth brome at the property.

The Impact of Invasives on the Home Garden

As a home gardener, it can be easy to overlook the damages that invasive plants cause. My previous garden was in an urban area where we were surrounded by irrigated yards, landscaping, and fairly well-maintained gardens. I had never experienced an invasive plant; my garden domain was small enough that I didn't comprehend how quickly these plants could spread out of control.

Moving to my more suburban neighborhood with larger lots, green spaces, open parks, and some unmanaged landscapes, I saw for the first time how invasives spread. As I became familiar with the invasive plants that had claimed our farm over the years, I started noticing them everywhere. The open-space greenbelt nearby was riddled with common buckthorn along the water's edge. Hoary cress had spread to the river down the street from the farm. Japanese knotweed and tree of heaven popped up along the length of our neighbor's agricultural ditch.

For many of us with smaller home properties or container gardens, invasive plants might not seem like a problem, but their impacts are felt in wild, unmanaged riparian and natural ecosystems. They quickly spread out of control in any location that lacks the funding and the people power required to keep invasive plants managed. Birds pick up seeds and berries and distribute them for miles, particularly berries from bush honeysuckle, oriental bittersweet, porcelain berry, and common buckthorn. Other invasive plants like butterfly bush create thousands of seeds per shrub, which can float on the wind far beyond their immediate planting space.

So while many gardeners tend to think that planting invasives isn't an issue in their own controlled space because they've never *seen* them spread, that does not mean the plants are not spreading. The aforementioned butterfly bush seeds, which float for miles, are highly viable germinators that typically take hold in unmanaged spaces. Kudzu is another famous example—originally sold to gardeners and municipalities as a fast-growing ornamental vine good for erosion control, it quickly spread in unmanaged spaces and now is killing old-growth forests. Invasives can seem like a nonissue for home gardeners, but in reality, the majority of invasive plant problems we have in North America today are a direct result of the horticulture industry pushing those plants to home gardeners and landscapers.

Invasive Plants for Sale

Many invasive plants—such as creeping bellflower, kudzu, English ivy, and multiflora rose—were brought here by the horticulture trade decades or even hundreds of years ago and have spread across the country. And while some are no longer sold due to their potential for ecosystem damage, many invasives are still on the market.

Gardeners are often surprised by the list of common invasive plants, because many of these plants are not only prevalent in landscaping plans, they are also frequently sold at nurseries, even in areas where they are declared invasive, and they are sold by online retailers without any declaration of their destructive potential. Most states have an official list of invasive plants—find yours and become familiar with it!

The discussion of invasive versus native plants is, of course, regional. What is invasive to one continent is native to another, but the importance of recognizing the difference is the same regardless of georegion.

For many of us with smaller gardens, invasive plants might not seem like a problem, but their impacts are felt in the wild.

Beautiful Alternatives to Common Invasives

Blue flax blooms in a meadow space and is an alternative to bachelor's button, which is invasive in my region.

Beautiful golden currant provides birds with berries and is an alternative to forsythia or burning bush.

Golden alexanders, native across North America, is an excellent alternative to the often-recommended sweet alyssum or the invasive Queen Anne's lace.

New Jersey tea is a native alternative to invasive butterfly bush and also has edible leaves.

Anise hyssop is a native alternative to purple loosestrife that feeds many pollinators and has a delicious flavor.

Rocky Mountain penstemon provides a beautiful and native alternative to creeping bellflower.

Commonly Sold Invasive Plants and Alternatives

Some of the most common invasive plants are sold in nurseries for use in home landscapes. Descriptions often include "rapid spreader," especially in regards to nonnative plants. Below are invasives common in North America with alternatives to try instead.

Invasive	Noninvasive Alternative
Bachelor's button	Blue flax, nodding onion, echinacea
Burning bush	Ninebark, currants
Butterfly bush/buddleia	Virginia sweetspire, New Jersey tea, viburnums
Chinese wisteria	American wisteria
Dame's rocket/sweet rocket	Perennial phlox
English ivy	Climbing hydrangea, mountain spurge, wild ginger
Japanese barberry	Ninebark, seven-son flower
Japanese honeysuckle	Black chokeberry
Oriental bittersweet	American bittersweet
Periwinkle	Moss phlox, mountain spurge, alpine strawberry
Purple loosestrife	Anise hyssop
Queen Anne's lace/ chocolate lace flower	Golden alexanders, yarrow
Sweet alyssum	Yerba mansa, field pussytoes, snow-in-summer, bunchberry
Sweet autumn clematis	Virgin's bower

There is significant difficulty in getting plants named to invasive lists. There are invasive plants that haven't officially been declared so in certain regions, but that doesn't mean they won't spread. It can take many years of spread before plants land on said lists; in the meantime, they create severe damage and it becomes too late to easily control them. Therefore, look at nationwide as well as state invasive lists and compare climate types. Does the plant clearly spread in many different climates? If so, it may be best to avoid it altogether.

Create a map of your garden site to think through the features of your space and plan how to reach your goals.

Planning the Garden Plantings

Creating a plan for a new garden or redoing an old one can quickly become overwhelming, even for a seasoned gardener! Early in my property conversion, I was advised to work in small sections each year, prepping other areas passively by layering them with mulch. It can be helpful to create a map of your existing lawn or garden space to identify pockets where native perennials and bird-supporting plants can be tucked in.

Create a Map

A map can help you think through the features of your garden space and envision how to reach your goals.

Identify structures and trees. Incorporate any structures or trees that might cast shade or compete with plants for water and sunlight. For example, large trees may cast dappled or full shade depending on the density of their leaves, and they frequently compete with undergrowth for water resources, so drought-tolerant shade lovers would be best utilized in those areas. Remember to estimate the mature sizes of these shrubs and trees, both in spread and height and the type of shade they will cast.

Plan for access. If your goal is to mix in production areas with perennial plantings, be sure to allocate space for pathways so you can transport amendments or cart out weeds. Paths can also create divisions within the garden that make planning out planting heights and spacing feel more natural.

Indicate soil types and moisture levels. Refer back to any evaluations you've conducted on

Planting for Climate Change

When evaluating plant selections for your garden, consider how the climate of your area has been changing in recent decades and how that may impact your perennial plants in particular. Most hardiness zones are becoming warmer, so be mindful of planting things that won't survive if that occurs. Water may become scarce in some areas, while flooding may become more frequent in others.

Depending on how your region's climate is shifting, planting drought-tolerant perennial plants, berming or mounding soil, and creating swales (areas of high and low elevation to capture water or create drainage) can help mitigate the changes. Even better, find plants that thrive in fluctuating temperatures and tolerate drought and occasional wet roots.

In my area, we have seen an increase in heavy storms and flooding, so when planting crops like lavender, which prefer dry soil, we have added soil berms to improve drainage.

Over the past couple of years, we have focused more on drought-tolerant perennials to help minimize our water needs—but this doesn't mean the garden can't look lush! Perennial asters, yarrow, echinacea, bee balm, anise hyssop, and native grasses form a thick and full landscape, needing very little, if any, additional water.

your soil. Flag where soil may be sandier or more compact, or where elevation changes dictate which types of plants will thrive with less effort.

It's more affordable and ecologically sound to plant things suited to your native soils and existing moisture levels, but you may wish to grow some plants that don't fit those parameters. Keep in mind that it's possible for soil to be regenerated, which in time will change what you can grow in a given area.

Creating a map of new bed areas can make gardening less expensive. I frequently hear gardeners complain that they had to start a bed over entirely because the wrong plant was put in the wrong location. Take your time to create a thorough plan based off your existing conditions, and plant for those conditions rather than trying to overhaul your entire garden's soil structure.

Our wooded area is unirrigated, which, given the tendency toward drought in our region, makes starting seeds and establishing plants there difficult. In areas where we are establishing seeds, such as the perennial, drought-tolerant blue grama seen here, we create small swales and berms to help channel and contain rainfall when it occurs.

6

Create Living Soil

ALLOWING LIVING ROOTS TO THRIVE in the soil is the key to a healthy soil food web. The longer we keep living roots in the soil, the longer we provide nourishment for that soil food web, and the healthier our soil will be in turn. Recall the soil food web and its foundation: The base layer is the roots of the plants themselves. Plant roots release root exudates for microbes, supporting the food chain of the whole garden ecosystem.

There are two main methods for supporting living roots in the soil: First, cover cropping adds living roots and organic matter to your garden beds; second, using no- or low-till methods to minimize soil disturbance keeps roots and their associated mycelial networks alive longer and introduces a wider array of biodiversity to support your garden plants.

Getting Started with Cover Crops

Cover crops serve a multitude of purposes in the garden, from erosion control to nutrient retention. They also provide organic matter and mulch to replenish depleted soils, help prevent weeds, and retain soil moisture. They can support biodiversity, leading to healthier soil and more pest and disease resistance in the garden.

A Solution for Unhealthy Soil

Before starting the farm, I always gardened in raised beds, layering expensive bagged soils on top of the existing clay. However, when we moved to the farm, we were overwhelmed with expenses, and our only option was to plant into the soil as it was. I remember looking down at the cracked, compacted soil, wondering if anything would grow in it. Perhaps it would? After all, the whole area had previously been produce farms, and our farm had once grown apples and watermelon. There had to be a way to make our dry chunks of heavy soil plantable.

While our first-year plants grew fine (although nothing to write home about), I started researching cover cropping. That first fall, I planted a cover crop of winter rye. I had no idea what I was doing or what my goals were other than better soil—but from what I had heard, cover crops would get me there. The rye germinated in fall, overwintered as dead blades of grasslike shoots, and took off in spring—and I mean *took off*! I had no plan for how to terminate the rye, and when planting time arrived, I was faced with what looked like a field of grass. As the rye continued to grow and flourish, I had to till it to kill the roots, or I would have had to apply an herbicide (not ideal) to get my field planted in time. In fact, I had to till *twice* to fully kill the rye. This was disappointing, considering I had planned to keep my beds no-till, but it worked: The cover crop was finally dead, and I could plant my seeds.

Farmhand Savannah tills the rye cover crop for a second time to terminate it after it began to regrow in the spring.

POSITIVE CHANGES IN THE FIRST YEAR

While that first round of cover cropping didn't go as hoped, I nonetheless noticed positive changes in the soil from just one season of that monoculture cover crop. That spring we had torrential rains—the kind frequently referred to as gully washers—not once but three times within a week. Other farmers in our city were pumping their fields with sump pumps and watching their topsoil and nutrients wash down storm drains. Meanwhile, the roots of that winter rye were holding our soil in place, safe from erosion.

I've come a long way since that first season of cover cropping, and I've learned that termination considerations are central to the decision of what cover crops to use, but the evidence of the process's benefits are ingrained in my brain. I have since made it a goal to have most areas of the farm covered with living roots for as much of the growing season as possible.

IT'S NOT ONE-SIZE-FITS-ALL

Cover cropping can be intimidating because there is no one-size-fits-all strategy—how to approach it is highly dependent on individual situations and soil needs. But the process is as simple as ordering seeds for a basic cover crop—one that will terminate easily, such as peas—and planting them, either in spring or fall (see the next section for a discussion of how to decide the best time to plant). As you gain experience with different crops and termination methods, you will feel more encouraged to experiment with different species and reap the benefits of a biodiverse mix.

These cover crop seeds contain a mix of 16 different types of plants to bring diversity to the soil ecosystem.

Cover Crops in the Home Garden

There's a misconception that cover cropping is for agricultural fields and not for home gardens, but this is absolutely not the case—every soil type can benefit from the practice! Cover crops can aerate and loosen heavy clay and improve moisture and nutrient retention in clay. They add organic matter to all types of soils, which is important in buffering pH (that is, bringing it closer to neutral) and providing a food source for the microbes to convert into energy for plants. In larger-scale farms, cover cropping involves a large tractor spreading seeds across a freshly tilled field, but in a garden, it's much simpler. Container gardens, in-ground beds, and even raised beds can be excellent candidates for cover cropping. The main considerations are (1) when and where do we plant the cover crop, (2) how do we terminate (kill) it, and (3) what do we plant?

When to Plant Cover Crops

In my experience, the most complicated part of cover cropping in the home garden has been timing. How do we grow a garden and still have time to cover crop? Most gardeners don't operate like large-scale farmers. There is no set harvest date for the entire crop, after which their beds are completely empty (though we will discuss this as an option and how to try it at home while still incorporating biodiversity). Typically cover cropping happens in either early spring or late summer. If your growing season is too short to allow cover cropping before or after your primary crop, undercropping may be a good option (see page 147). Each method has pros and cons.

LATE-SUMMER/FALL COVER CROPPING

Late summer into early fall is my preferred time to cover crop, as it requires the least amount of management and effort in spring when the garden is full of other tasks to accomplish. While the timing to get the cover crop grown in enough to provide sufficient amounts of organic matter and nitrogen is a bit tricky, with general knowledge of last frost dates, it can be much easier than spring cover cropping for a few reasons.

Warmer weather. The weather is typically more reliable in fall. While in spring we often deal with errant late frosts, potential spring snows, and cold soil temperatures, fall usually offers warm temperatures and somewhat more predictable weather.

Hairy vetch forms a mat that makes excellent mulch while fixing nitrogen, but it can reseed and become invasive if not terminated at the right time.

Soil temperature. At this time of year, soil temperatures are warmer, so seeds germinate more readily, and it's easier to irrigate without the risk of unexpected freezing.

Easy termination. If you select cover crops that will winter-kill, or die off, in the cold winter temperatures of your hardiness zone, termination is much less work, as you don't have to do anything beyond planting. The cover plants will grow until late fall/early winter, die off with the cold, and leave your beds ready for planting into in spring. Which varieties winterkill in your region obviously depends on how cold your winter gets.

The downside of late-summer/fall cover crops is that you have to terminate your garden before the first frost to sow the seeds, but there are ways to navigate that as well, such as interplanting/undercropping (see page 147).

SPRING COVER CROPPING

Spring cover cropping has its own benefits and challenges.

Longer fall garden season. One advantage is that your garden can continue growing until frost in fall instead of being cleared to plant a cover crop; a late-summer cover crop requires earlier termination of your garden plants. The extended garden season is ideal if you have productive plants you aren't ready to remove from the garden or that improve if left until after frost (such as kale and carrots, which grow sweeter after being hit by frost).

Mulch for planting. Another advantage of an early-spring cover crop is that if the crop is allowed to grow long enough, it will usually leave the garden with a healthy amount of mulch after termination that can be used to support your spring planting. When a cover crop is planted in fall and dies back over winter, much of this organic matter breaks down during winter and spring, and just a light covering of mulch remains when it's time to plant. A spring cover crop will provide plenty of mulch for the coming season, depending on how you choose to terminate.

Timing. The downsides of planting a garden cover crop in early spring include difficulties with timing and weather. If your growing zone is anything like mine, you may frequently get unexpected late-spring snows, and in shady areas that snow may hang around the garden until late in spring. If this is the case, be prepared to cover the growing cover crop with some burlap to protect it from hard freezes, and avoid planting to spring cover crop in shady areas that stay frozen solid until late spring.

Crop selection. To make your cover crop selection, first consider your goals for your cover crop: nitrogen fixation? biodiversity? weed suppression? Then think carefully about germination and termination: The crop must be able to germinate in the cold soil temperatures of early spring, and then you'll want crops you can terminate easily, without equipment—ideally ones that can be killed by cutting or crimping down at the root, such as peas. Keep in mind that your crop won't be winter-killed by frost and cold temperatures like a fall-sown cover crop.

Waiting period. You'll need to allow a week or two between the termination of your cover crop and the planting of your production plants to ensure the spring-planted cover crop is dead and beginning break down before new seedlings go into the ground.

FULL-SEASON COVER CROPPING

While most of us home gardeners are typically trying to cram as much into our garden beds as possible and are usually unwilling to give entire gardens over to cover cropping for a whole season, doing so can be a quick and beneficial way to heal soil. Growing (and terminating) several rounds of cover crops in a season can add organic matter, reduce compaction, and develop a vibrant and diverse soil food web—and can be very helpful for extremely poor soils. It may be worth considering dedicating some garden space to a full year of cover crops, particularly if the soil is very poor.

Where to Plant Cover Crops

I think of planting cover crops as "growing mulch." Doing so helps me to understand the timing and placement of cover crops in garden beds: either under and around plants, or before and after plants.

INTERPLANTING/UNDERCROPPING

One of my favorite cover-cropping methods is interplanting, or undercropping. This means we plant cover crops while our production plants are still growing. This is convenient for home gardeners, as most of us hesitate to pull out our favorite plants before the first frost.

A mixed cover crop of various species grows under beans at the end of the garden season.

These late-summer tomatoes, peppers, kale, and rosemary are trimmed and ready for an underplanted cover crop.

Underplanting a cover crop allows us to still get a full season's harvest from our plants while reaping the benefits of cover cropping.

So how do we keep those plants and cover crop at the same time? The process starts in mid to late August, six to eight weeks before the average first frost. We begin cutting back and thinning out unhealthy plants and leaves, many of which are starting to fade by that point in the garden season. Tomatoes and kale get a trim of the lower leaves, sprawling plants are staked up, and plants that are diseased or struggling are removed. This process usually results in patches of sunlight-exposed soil that we can then seed. Avoid planting cover crops around plants too early in the season, which can lead to the leaching of nutrients and moisture away from your main production plants.

DEDICATED COVER CROP BEDS

Another alternative is to have two (or more) garden beds, one dedicated to early-summer plants (radish, lettuce, brassicas, sweet pea, snapdragon, herbs that bolt with later heat, etc.) and another for late-summer producers (tomato, squash, bean, pumpkin, pepper, dahlia, zinnia, etc.). While still creating lots of biodiversity in each bed, separating early (cool-temperature) and late (warm-temperature) producers means you can plan on cover cropping the cool-temperature production bed in late summer, after those plants have ceased production and faded with the oncoming summer heat. The entire bed can be cleared and planted all at once rather than interplanted with still-producing plants.

The bed for warm-temperature producers, meanwhile, can be planted in early spring (before the last frost) with a cover crop and terminated a couple of weeks after the last frost once soil temperatures are nice and warm for planting those heat-loving, late-summer producers.

Using this method, each bed gets a cover crop, but the crops are staggered. If you choose to use this method, change which bed produces the late-summer and early-summer plants each season to ensure good crop rotation.

How to Plant Cover Crops

Despite our farm being more than an acre, I don't have special planting equipment. Instead, I usually broadcast my cover crop seeds manually, first gently loosening the surface inch or two of soil by hand or with a hand rake, then sprinkling seeds and raking them in until lightly covered. Finally, I cover the bed with a thin layer of homemade compost and a thin mulch of finely chopped leaves, garden debris, or pine shavings. Avoid wood chips as a mulch for cover crops; they are usually too thick for the seeds to germinate and grow through.

If you are in a very dry climate and use irrigation or drip tubing to water your beds, dig a small trench alongside the tubes and sprinkle in the cover crop seeds before covering the tubes rather than broadcasting the seeds. This can help you conserve the quantity of seed needed and make for a better germination rate.

Terminating Cover Crops

One of the biggest mistakes I see home gardeners make when they first plant cover crops is failing to consider how they will terminate (or kill) the crop before the next growing season.

There are several ways to terminate cover crops. But regardless of which method you choose, it's important to research your chosen cover crop and identify your preferred method of termination *before* sowing it in the garden! Making the wrong selection could result in a messy fix.

TILLING

Tilling is the process of turning the soil under and chopping up both roots and aboveground plants. The benefits include helping control weeds (except rhizome-based ones) and making direct seeding easier by loosening the soil surface. Tillage is effective at terminating most cover crops; however, it results in a lot of soil disturbance, to the detriment of the fungi, bacteria, arthropods, and other soil life. It can also lead to erosion if done repeatedly, because loosened soil can wash or blow away with exposure to weather. While tillage often gets a bad reputation, I don't like the idea of ruling it out altogether. It is a useful tool for starting a garden bed from existing grass as described in the section on the native soil method (see page 59) or terminating a difficult-to-kill cover crop (like our rye!), and it can be a good alternative to using herbicide. But the aim should be to use it sparingly and never as part of routine management.

CRIMPING

Crimping involves pressing down a crop at the flowering stage, bending the stem enough to halt the growth of the plant. The goal is to bend the stem enough to stop the flow of nutrients to the top of the plant, effectively killing it without the risk of it blowing away. In my low-tech garden,

Using a small electric tiller to terminate a cover crop can work if the plants are small enough, but if there is more growth, a larger machine will be needed to avoid jamming the tiller.

A bucket of oats, peas, buckwheat, and radish is ready to be sown as a cover crop in a garden bed.

CRIMPING TO TERMINATE **COVER CROPS**

Set up the device by tying a piece of rope to either end of an angle iron or a heavy piece of lumber.

Hold the rope firmly with both hands, standing upright.

Use one foot to press into the cover crop while the other foot shuffles behind.

I simply use my hands or a piece of angle iron attached to a rope to press down on the stems. This technique results in very little soil disturbance and, if done correctly, has no negative impact on the soil life (unless the cover crop is sown too thickly, which can create too thick of a layer after crimping and smother some aerobic microbes—but this is rare in my experience).

Larger farms use tractor-driven crimpers and rollers. On a small scale, this can be done with a 3-foot piece of angle iron, which provides sufficient weight and a sharp edge to help crimp the stems. Attach a rope to each end of the angle iron and hold the rope by the ends near your waist, lifting the iron and pressing it down with one foot while stepping along the cover crop with the other foot. To be effective, press down with the full weight of your body to fully crimp the stem.

This crimped cover crop of oats and peas has died back and is ready to plant into. You can also crimp by hand by grabbing and bending the crop or stomping on it.

You can also crimp by hand, if your garden is small enough—simply grab and forcefully bend the crop down, or stomp on it. Even though my garden space is quite large, I often use this method because it is convenient, especially if I'm interplanting/undercropping a cover crop with a producing plant, such as the buckwheat I interplant with my dahlias.

Crimping is an excellent method for supporting soil health, but it is fairly labor intensive and requires longer growth periods than may be desirable in the home garden. For crimping to be an effective termination method, it has to be done at just the right stage of growth—typically at the cover crop's flowering stage—and will only work with certain varieties of cover crops. Cover crops that cannot be terminated using this method include grasslike varieties such as annual rye (the stems are too flexible and soft to terminate by crimping) and the sorghum-Sudan grass hybrid.

Cutting is another method for terminating a cover crop, as with these oats and peas, which I hand cut with a sickle.

CUTTING

Also known as "chop and drop," this is a simple method to attempt at home. It can be done with a weed whacker, sickle, or even a lawnmower. In this method, the cover crop is terminated at soil level and the residue is left on the surface of the soil. Only certain cover crops can be terminated by this method, and the cutting needs to be done at the correct stage—typically flowering stage, or regrowth will occur. For example, chop and drop can work well for the nitrogen-fixing hairy vetch, but it must take place when the plant is blooming. If done earlier, the plant will grow back. Similarly, if crops are cut too late after blooming, they may go to seed and cause problems later (hairy vetch can be very persistent and create a mess in the garden if allowed to go to seed).

Laying a tarp over a crimped cover crop assists in termination.

SMOTHERING

Smothering involves applying a clear or black plastic tarp over the cover crop (either after cutting it down or while crop is still small) to ensure it dies off. This is a low-effort means of termination. A clear tarp will heat and terminate

Hairy vetch (left) is cold tolerant and will not winter kill in most of North America, so it is essential to have a termination plan if using it as a cover crop. This mixed sowing of peas and oats (right) is cold tolerant but will ultimately die at the first hard freeze.

better than a black one, because the sunlight reaches the soil and heats it more. Typically the tarp needs to be left in place for about two weeks in sunny weather to kill the cover crop. This method can be a very good backup plan in case your first method of termination fails! The downsides are that it can kill some of the soil life in the top inch or two of soil (though this will regenerate fairly quickly), it requires a fair amount of plastic that will inevitably end up in a landfill, and it can be difficult to do on a small scale if you are interplanting your cover crop among existing plants or perennials.

WINTER-KILLING

This is my favorite method of termination (possibly due to my laziness in tending cover crops in spring with everything else I have to nurse along at that time of year). I like a cover crop that I can sow in late summer or early fall that will simply die off on its own once the temperatures reach a certain low. Winter-killing doesn't require soil disturbance or additional plastic or equipment, and it leaves a protective blanket over the soil for the winter months that breaks down into a remaining layer of mulch protection for spring plantings.

Herbicide

Many large-scale farmers terminate their cover crops with herbicide. This is not something I recommend. Repeated use of herbicides can lead to herbicide-resistant weeds and have detrimental impacts on the soil microbes and earthworm populations. It is, however, a method many use for termination in the regenerative agriculture space and requires serious consideration. If you select an herbicide termination, be sure to only target your cover crop and to research accurate application rates and timing.

This method requires good timing to ensure that the plants are large enough at winterkill time to provide enough soil cover and be worth the effort they took to seed. Be sure to select a crop that will winter-kill in your climate.

ALWAYS HAVE A TERMINATION PLAN

It's vital to consider what tools and techniques you feel comfortable using to terminate before selecting your cover crop and to make sure the crop you choose is compatible with this plan.

How to terminate. How I'm going to kill my cover crop is one of the first things I consider, because I prefer not to till my garden soil if possible. I also don't spray herbicides. I prefer cutting, winter-killing, smothering, or crimping.

In my opinion, crops that require crimping work best in warmer growing zones with longer gardening seasons, where gardeners can delay spring plantings and still have good harvests. This method is less ideal for shorter growing seasons like mine, where reaching a good stage for crimping typically means I'd have to plant much later than normal. That being said, crimping followed by smothering with a tarp will kill the cover crop even if it's not at the ideal stage for termination.

When to terminate. When to terminate is as important as how. With some varieties, if we try to kill too early, the crop will simply regrow. If termination occurs too late (typically after the flowering stage), we risk losing benefits like nitrogen fixation, as the plant puts the nitrogen it accumulated in the roots into seed production. Wait even longer, and those seeds will become viable, drop on the ground, and create a potentially huge mess!

Prepare a backup plan. Be sure to have a backup plan if the method you first planned fails to kill the cover crop. Typically, for my garden, smothering is the backup. If our winter is milder than normal and doesn't get quite cold enough to terminate our cover crop, or if we get regrowth in spring that I wasn't planning for, I throw a tarp over the area and weigh it down around the sides to ensure that the crop is dead before I plant.

PLANTING AFTER TERMINATION

After terminating the cover crop, a rest period is needed. This both ensures that the crop is dead and won't regrow and prevents potential nutrient tie-up while the soil microbes use existing nitrogen to break down the carbon in the cover crop plants' roots. With most termination methods, two weeks should be enough time before planting. Of course, no wait period is needed for winter-killed cover crops, because the crop will be dead long before planting time.

Choose a Cover Crop Based on Your Garden Goals

Cover crops can help with nitrogen fixation (see the next section) and nitrogen scavenging (keeping the existing nitrogen in the soil from washing away); smothering weeds; increasing biodiversity; building organic matter; reducing erosion; and even protecting against soil-dwelling pests like grubs and root knot nematodes. But not all cover crops serve all purposes, so identifying your garden goals is a helpful way to narrow down seed selection.

NITROGEN FIXING

Nitrogen is the soil nutrient plants need most, and frequently it must be added. Many gardeners rely on synthetic fertilizers for a nitrogen boost, but it's possible to add this vital growth component to soil via a cover crop that fixes nitrogen. Nitrogen fixation is the process in which certain plants draw nitrogen from the air and fix (attach) it into their roots via associations with soil bacteria and microorganisms. If you pull up a plant that has been fixing atmospheric nitrogen into its roots, you'll see nitrogen nodules, which can look like small whiteish lumps on the roots. The correct soil rhizobia must be present for nitrogen fixation to occur. Since these rhizobia may or may not be present in the soil, many experts recommend applying the correct inoculant for the cover crop seed to ensure nitrogen fixation. Inoculants typically come in a dry

Small white nitrogen nodules on the roots of this pea cover crop indicate that the soil contains the rhizobia necessary to enable nitrogen fixation.

powder form that is applied to seeds and wetted to achieve good coverage before planting.

When planting a cover crop with the goal of nitrogen fixation, termination timing is key. Terminate too early, and the plants won't have time to grow large enough to pull enough nitrogen from the air to make a difference in fertilizer needs. Terminate too late, and the plant will start using the nitrogen stores it has created to form its own seeds. For best benefits, terminate a nitrogen-fixing cover crop at the flowering stage (or just prior), before the flowers begin to change to seedpods.

A bed that has grown a crop of particularly heavy feeders (think corn, squash, and tomatoes) may need a good nitrogen-fixing cover crop to replenish nutrients those plants have taken from the soil. Typically, I'm ready to be done with squash and have harvested corn by late summer, but the tomatoes are still going. Removing the remaining corn and squash while pruning up the lower leaves of the tomato lets me fit in a cover crop (for my zone, this means late August or early September).

Nitrogen-fixing cover crops include legumes such as peas, hairy vetch, lentils, and clovers.

If I Plant Legumes in the Garden, Am I Getting Nitrogen from Them?

If you plant a crop of peas and then follow it with heavy feeders, like tomatoes, will the peas fix nitrogen to feed the tomatoes?

They might, but only if you don't harvest them. I've heard gardeners told they can get a harvest of peas, then chop down the pea plants and reap the benefits of nitrogen fixation in the soil. This is incorrect! While chopping and leaving the plants on the soil surface after pea harvest will provide a bit of nitrogen via the organic matter breakdown, the fact is that the plant will have used up its nitrogen reserves to produce the peas you picked. So, no, you cannot have a pea harvest and reap the nitrogen fixation benefits of the plant for the following crop. If you plant peas and terminate them at the flowering stage (before harvest), then the plan will work.

WEED SMOTHERING

Gardening in weedy areas can be exceptionally challenging! We have one row of garden beds adjacent to a neighbor who struggles to keep weeds under control, and often the seeds of those undesirable plants blow over our fence. In these beds, we like to use a thick layer of cover crops, including one with weed-smothering ability. Any cover crop can reduce the amount of weeds seen in the garden via competition for space as well as simply by preventing weed seeds from reaching the soil and germinating, especially if the cover crop is sown thickly. But there are also certain cover crops that have allelopathic tendencies; that is, they prevent other plants from growing near them by releasing compounds that inhibit growth or prevent germination.

Allelopathic cover crops can sometimes have unintended effects. For example, if you grow an allelopathic cover crop and later attempt to direct sow a plant such as radish in the same bed, there may be some negative effects on germination. The strength of the germination effect is related to seed size: Smaller seeds will be more negatively affected than larger seeds. To avoid affecting your later plantings, terminate allelopathic cover crops a couple of weeks prior to planting.

Allelopathic/weed-smothering cover crops include cereal rye/winter cereal grains; sorghums; brassicas such as rapeseed, mustard, and radish; and buckwheat.

INCREASING SOIL BIODIVERSITY

Cover cropping is an excellent way to introduce biodiversity, which is a key part of the regenerative garden. It reduces the impact of diseases and pests and attracts a wider and more diverse range of organisms to the soil food web, bringing the ecosystem more into balance.

I'm examining tips of a wheat cover crop that is about to set seed, to see if it's ready for termination. It is planted in a daffodil bed in order to protect soil from erosion and smother weeds after the blooms finish.

This diverse cover crop is nearly ready for termination. Notice the development of flowers.

A cover crop of oats and peas peeks through a layer of spring snow and will continue growing once temperatures warm.

Any mix of cover crops will help with this goal. In fact, the more the merrier! I've done cover crop sowings containing 12 or more different varieties. However, while incorporating more varieties will result in greater biodiversity, it can also make for complicated termination considerations, so be prepared with a backup plan for termination.

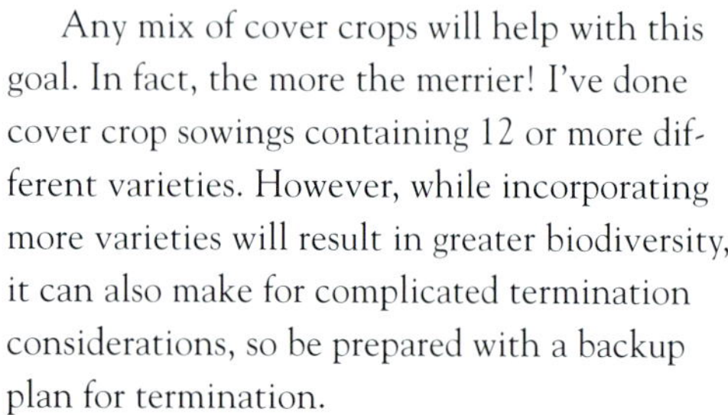

We have used a mix with squash, sunflower, millet, radish, cowpea, oat, buckwheat, mustard, sorghum-Sudan grass, Sunn hemp, flax, clover, and black bean to build soil and introduce biodiversity where we are establishing new gardens. While most of these varieties winter-killed in my climate (USDA Zone 5/6), the clover came back in full force in spring, requiring us to hastily throw down a tarp and resulting in a delayed planting in that bed.

Using a diverse cover crop mix can be an excellent approach, but it is still wise to research the individual components of a mix or start out with fewer seeds in your mixes as you learn the qualities (and termination methods) of each.

BUILDING ORGANIC MATTER/ REDUCING EROSION

The presence of organic matter is essential to ongoing soil health—it significantly improves the soil's ability to retain nutrients, helps retain moisture (and reduce swings in moisture levels), breaks up clay soils, and assists with the water-holding capacity of sandy soil. Organic matter provides a food source for bacteria and fungi, making for a healthier soil food web that is better able to break down nutrients and make them available for plants. High levels of organic material in soil also help protect our watersheds by reducing nutrient runoff.

While many gardeners attempt to increase their soil organic matter by adding lots of compost, one of the most affordable (and fastest) ways to build organic matter is through cover cropping. Cover crops build organic matter both by reducing erosion and by adding biomass to the soil via roots underground and green growth above.

Any cover crop will help add organic matter to the soil—grasses and brassicas tend to add the most but can be the most difficult to terminate.

FIGHTING SOIL-DWELLING PESTS

Increasing overall biodiversity improves the garden's ability to ward off pest damage, and cover crops are a quick tool to assist.

Manage pests like root knot nematodes (which can spread and damage roses, dahlias, potatoes, and more) with a cover crop such as Sunn hemp or sorghum-Sudan grass, which can produce allelopathic substances against them. In contrast, other cover crops (cowpeas in particular) increase the possibility of sustaining a root

To help combat soil-dwelling pests, we interplant with different plants including miniature marigolds; this petite variety is 'Starfire' mix.

These turnips were grown as a cover crop to help loosen a heavy clay soil area.

knot population over winter and even encouraging their population growth.

Beware, however, that certain cover crops can exacerbate the presence of soil-dwelling pests. Wireworm, for example, may worsen in gardens planted with grassy cover crops such as sorgum-Sudan grass or winter rye. If you have a soil-dwelling pest, research your planned cover crop first to ensure it is a good fit to help solve the problem.

Marigolds can reduce pests, according to some studies. In our first year, we planted roses in several areas of the farm. Most did well, but there was one spot where three rosebushes died in one season. After pulling up the roots, we saw clear evidence of root knot nematodes. Whether they were already in the soil or came in on the roses we bought, we aren't sure, but we pulled those roses out along with the others in the area and grew marigolds there the following year. Marigolds, particularly the French varieties, produce the allelochemical alpha-terthienyl, which helps reduce populations of root-knot nematodes (along with 14 genera of other plant-parasitic nematodes) and possibly other plant pests such as fungi, bacteria, and insects. This area required a full growing season to remediate, and it seemed to help (though without pulling up all the roses, we can't be sure). For now, the roses are doing well.

REDUCING COMPACTION

When we try to reclaim an area of the garden that has become heavily compacted over time, especially an area with clay soil, we use root-vegetable cover crops like daikon radish and turnip combined with a couple of inches of compost (assuming it's not a high-phosphorus location) to quickly add organic matter and create gaps in the soil for that compost to work down into. If we seed the cover crops in late summer and give them a chance to grow until freeze, they will often decompose over winter. The holes left by the radishes fill in with the compost, resulting in aeration with no need to work the soil.

NITROGEN SCAVENGING

If your soil has a high amount of nitrogen (say you applied aged manure in the late summer or grew a nitrogen-fixing cover crop over summer), it can be a good idea to plant a nitrogen-scavenging cover crop to hold that nitrogen in place in the soil until spring. Nitrogen *fixing* and nitrogen *scavenging* are different functions. Nitrogen leaches from soil easily, so planting a nitrogen-scavenging crop in late summer can be particularly helpful if you have sandy soil or wet winters/springs, which can result in the runoff of nutrients.

Nitrogen-scavenging cover crops include cereal rye, sorghum-Sudan grass, and radish.

Cover Crop Options by Goal/Type/Winterkill

While there are many cover crop options, the ones included here are most easily managed and unlikely to become invasive or weedy.

Common Name	Botanical Name	Winterkill USDA Zone	Best Planted *	Soil Temp for Germination	Fixes Nitrogen	Scavenges Excess Nitrogen	Chokes Out Weeds	Good for Beneficial Insects	Erosion Control
Alfalfa	*Medicago sativa*	5 and below	Late summer to early fall	34°F [1°C]	++++	+	++	++	+++
Annual ryegrass	*Lolium multiflorum*	3 and below	Late summer to fall	40°F [4°C]		++++	++		++++
Common buckwheat	*Fagopyrum esculentum*	Frost kills	Spring or late summer	50°F [10°C]		+	++++	++++	+
Common sunflower	*Helianthus annuus*	Frost kills	Spring to summer	60°F [16°C]		+++	+	++++	++++
Common wheat	*Triticum aestivum*	4 and below	Late summer to early fall	38°F [3°C]		+++	+++		++++
Crimson clover	*Trifolium incarnatum*	5 and below	Late summer to early fall	42°F [6°C]	++++	+	++	+++	+++
Fava bean	*Vicia faba*	7 and below	Late summer	55°F [13°C]	+++	+	++	+++	++
Field pea, winter pea	*Pisum sativum* subsp. *arvense*	6 and below	Late summer to early fall	41°F [5°C]	+++	+	++	++	++
Hairy vetch	*Vicia villosa*	4 and below	Late summer to early fall	60°F [16°C]	++++	+	+++	+++	++
Oat, spring oat	*Avena sativa*	7 and below	Late summer to early fall	38°F [3°C]		+++	++++	+	+++
Radish, oil-seed radish, daikon	*Raphanus sativus*	6 and below	Late summer to early fall	45°F [7°C]		++++	+++	++	+
Sorghum-Sudan grass	*Sorghum bicolor* var. *sudanese*	Frost kills	Summer	65°F [18°C]		++++	++++		++++
Turnip, forage turnip	*Brassica rapa*	6 and below	Late summer to early fall	45°F [7°C]		+++	+++	++	+

* You can plant outside of these times; however, if planting in spring or summer, be sure to terminate before the cover crop sets seed.

Creates Large Amount of Organic Matter	Good for Animal Grazing	Best Used with Inoculant	Recommended Termination	
++++	++++	Y	Winter-kill, till	"Dormant" varieties of alfalfa will often overwinter and not winter-kill, so be cautious with variety if using winterkill as termination. Can cause bloat in livestock.
++++	++++		Till (multiple passes may be required), tarp	Good shade tolerance. Not tolerant of drought and heat. Not as winter hardy as cereal rye. Can be difficult to terminate.
++			Winter-kill (check zone), till, tarp	Excellent at attracting beneficials; rapid growth in short time. Do not let go to seed to prevent weediness.
++			Winter-kill (annual)	Excellent at remediating contaminated soils and attracting birds and beneficials. Improves compaction. Best if allowed to flower, remove before setting seed if reseeding is not desired (or harvest seeds for consumption).
+++	++++		Crimp, till (multiple passes may be required)	Good shade and drought tolerance. Best if planted in late summer/fall.
++++	++++	Y	Crimp, winter-kill (check zone), till	Good shade, heat, and drought tolerance. Can cause bloat in livestock.
+++	++	Y	Mow, winter-kill (check zone), crimp, till	Forms mycorrhizal associations in soils and increases soil phosphorus availability. Can be used to break garden disease cycles. Shoots are edible.
++	++	Y	Crimp, mow, winter-kill (check zone), till, tarp	Do not plant before crops sensitive to fusarium (such as lisianthus). Shoots are edible.
+++		Y	Mow, crimp, till (multiple passes may be required), winter-kill (check zone)	Good shade and drought tolerance. Can become aggressively weedy if allowed to go to seed. Can be a host for root knot nematode. Can cause bloat in livestock.
+++	++++		Crimp, winter-kill (check zone), till, tarp	Best as a late-winter cover crop. Nearly always winter-kills. Not tolerant of drought. Can harvest oats and use for herbal applications.
+++	+++		Winter-kill (check zone), till	Good heat and drought tolerance. Can attract flea beetles.
++++	+++		Winter-kill (check zone), till	Excellent heat and drought tolerance. Often used to battle soil-dwelling nematodes like root knot nematode.
+	++++		Winter-kill (check zone), till	Better heat tolerance. May not winter-kill if heavy snowcover persists over winter.

Cover cropping can seem intimidating when you first start out. But remember, in the worst-case scenario, you can tarp and smother out any crops that have gone awry, so get experimenting! Not only will cover crops bring biodiversity to the garden and make soil healthier, they will get you thinking about your soil's health in new ways. Assess any empty spots in the garden and consider whether there is time in your gardening schedule to get a decent cover crop going (especially in late summer). If so, have seed on hand and go for it!

What's my cover-crop formula? In my Zone 5/6 climate, I like to use a mixed cover crop of buckwheat, field peas (with an inoculant for nitrogen fixation), and oats, which grows in by frost and continues to grow after, finally terminating when temperatures cool and the ground freezes. This leaves organic matter, nitrogen, and a mulch layer that's ready to go for spring planting. If your ground does not freeze over winter, you will need to plan for alternative termination.

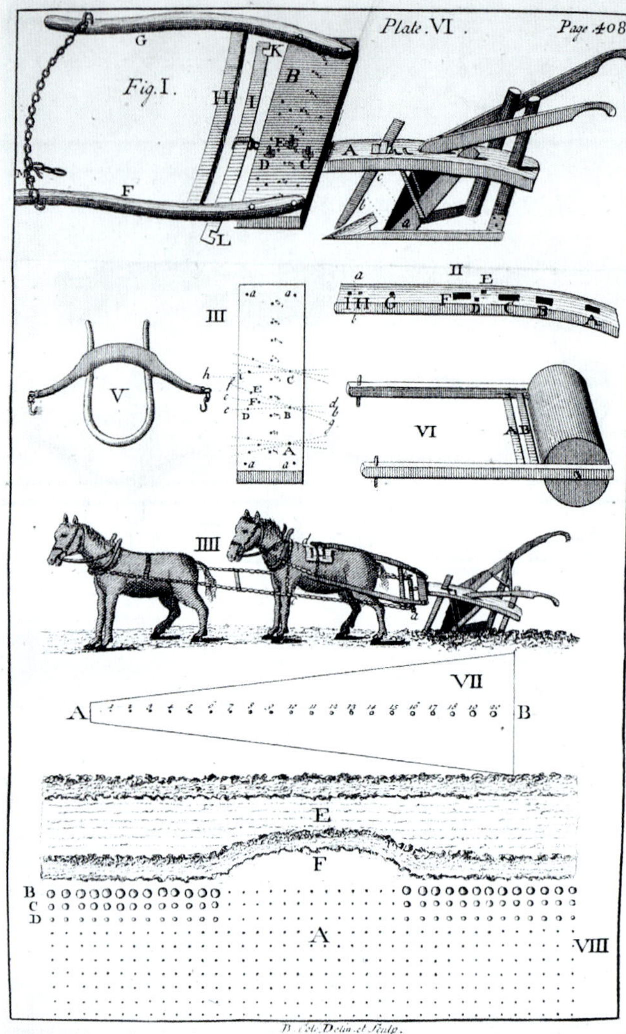

In the 1700s, Jethro Tull espoused the idea of tilling the soil in his Horse-Hoeing Husbandry, *with illustrations such as this one demonstrating how to use horses for turning over the soil.*

Minimize Soil Disturbance with No-Till Methods

Tillage has long been practiced in North America, often to the great detriment of the topsoil. While there are times when tilling is appropriate, for the most part it harms soil health and is best to avoid in the regenerative garden.

A History of Tillage in North America

When European settlers first started spreading across the great prairies of North America and establishing homesteads, they used ox-drawn plows to turn over the thick, rich soil. Prior to this, the soil was undisturbed—Indigenous peoples did not practice such turning of the soil. The idea of tillage harkens back to the agriculturist Jethro Tull in 1700s England. He theorized that plant roots had mouths that actually consumed tiny pieces of soil, and therefore the soil needed to be pulverized into smaller pieces in order for the plants to be able to uptake the soil nutrients. In his 1731 book *Horse-Hoeing Husbandry: Or, an Essay on the Principles of Vegetation and Tillage*, Tull wrote, "For the finer land is made by tillage, the richer will it become, and the more plants it will maintain. . . . I am in no doubt, that any soil (be it rich or poor) can ever be made too fine by tillage."

In the 1800s, these assertions were questioned in other papers, including D. Lee's 1849 article "The Philosophy of Tillage" and H. J. Water's 1888 report "Relation of Tillage to Soil Conservation." Water observed increased soil erosion and decline in crop yield following tillage, and Lee reported that crop yields decreased over time with tillage due to the "oxidation and loss of soil organic matter."

SOIL LOSS DURING THE DUST BOWL ERA

In the United States, the Dust Bowl of the 1930s was a direct result of over-tillage. Combined with the effects of a prolonged drought, farmers who insisted on tilling their fields saw their topsoil all but blow away. During the Dust Bowl period, farmers lost an average of 20 tons of topsoil per acre, per year. The Soil Conservation Service (SCS; now the National Resources Conservation Services) was formed in 1935 as an agency of the US Department of Agriculture to address the impact of soil health on the country's economy and ecology. The SCS aimed to educate farmers across the country on soil conservation methods, including reduced tillage, to assist with the impacts of soil erosion. Still, nearly a century later, many farmers continue to farm using annual tillage and soil disturbance. While topsoil losses aren't as disastrous as the Dust Bowl numbers, topsoil is still being lost at an average of around 7.6 tons per acre annually. In contrast, topsoil can be regrown at a rate of approximately 0.5 tons per acre.

Why to Avoid Tillage in Home Gardens

While this may seem like a problem unique to farms and croplands, our gardens are subject to these same rates of erosion and degradation when overworked. Many of us have heard that frequent working and turning of the soil is bad—but do we fully understand why? As we learn more about the interactions of the soil food web and the billions of lives that exist within the soil, incredible research has been done on what happens when we disturb that delicate ecosystem.

Close to the soil surface, where there are porous spaces, gaps, and holes within the soil, live the aerobic, or oxygen-needing, bacteria and

A house stands surrounded by depleted topsoil in the midst of the Dust Bowl of the 1930s, brought about in part by the widespread overuse of tillage.

fungi. Farther down in the deeper layers of the more compacted soil are anaerobic bacteria—the life that doesn't need as much oxygen to thrive and survive (see page 39).

Disturbing the soil through deep tillage or turning of our garden soil causes a lot of damage, exposing the anaerobic life to excess oxygen while suffocating the aerobic life. This can result in massive die-off of soil life: By turning and disturbing the ground, we expose this soil life to UV rays that can kill it, and we dry out the soil, which makes the soil life more vulnerable. While already healthy soil can regenerate its soil food web over time, the less we do to disturb it, and the less frequently we do it, the better.

When Is Soil Disturbance Appropriate?

When is soil disturbance acceptable in the regenerative garden? For many of us with very compacted or heavy clay soils, it can sometimes be impossible to get a seed to take or to establish any kind of plant life to sustain the soil microbes. Tillage can be a helpful tool when creating a new bed, particularly if you aren't able to make enough compost on-site to use lasagna or no-dig methods.

A one-time till to establish beds is sometimes the best choice. I tilled this new garden bed from an area that was previously grass.

In the native soil method of starting garden beds, which begins with tilling the soil to help remove existing vegetation (except in cases of rhizome-based weeds) or prepare soil that has been compacted for a long period, a bed is tilled *only* when it is established; then it is maintained by no-till methods, including planting a cover crop to help replenish the soil life and to add organic matter.

Other common methods of working the soil, such as manual turning with a shovel to work in compost or amendments, also count as soil disturbance. Even this simple act, if done too aggressively or too often, can lead to the breakdown of soil aggregation and life.

While it can seem counterintuitive to recommend a one-time till to establish a garden bed, it can be similarly argued that any method of garden bed establishing damages the soil. Laying down cardboard or thick layers of soils and composts can suffocate existing soil life. Occultation can kill soil life via high temperatures and results in plastic waste. Sod cutting removes organic matter. Each method is a tool to getting your garden established, and it is up to the gardener to determine which method is most appropriate for their own scenario.

Once a bed is established, the regenerative practices in this guide, including cover cropping and mulching, should make annual working and tillage of the soil unnecessary. Should you find your soil heavy or still compacted in the early stages of adopting regenerative and ecological gardening practices, consider broadforking.

BROADFORKING

Broadforks resemble garden forks, with large tines coming down from a wide metal base and handles on either side to grip. The gardener steps on the wide base, working back and forth using bodyweight to push the tines into the soil, and then pulls back gently on the handles until the soil just cracks but does not get turned over. These breaks in the soil surface let oxygen and

Using a broadfork to aerate soil in a new garden bed area before planting will help lighten the soil and allow roots access to oxygen.

surface organic matter enter, helping to create pockets of air and gently lightening the soil without heavy soil life disturbance.

I often see the broadfork used incorrectly, more like a shovel, with the gardener pulling the tool back so far that the soil is lifted from the earth and flipped. This is an improper use of the broadfork—if a gardener wants to turn soil, a shovel would be a better tool.

If I plan to broadfork an area of the garden, it is typically because it is compacted, indicating a lack of organic matter. If I have a batch of good homemade organic compost, I'll sprinkle a thin ¼- to ½-inch layer over the surface prior to (or after) broadforking to help work some of those organic matter particles and microbes down into the soil more quickly without doing a full tillage or turning of the soil.

Broadforks can be costly. In a small garden, you can use a basic garden fork to a similar effect, inserting the tines into the soil and pulling back gently. But if you have large gardens, investing in a broadfork will make the process go more quickly. Broadforks with metal handles last longer than those with wooden handles, especially in clay soil, and are worth the extra expense.

This light working of the soil for aeration and organic matter addition can be done in spring (once the soil is dry enough to work) or in fall, after the addition of any organic matter. In spring, broadforking can be done before planting to lighten compacted soils and thus make planting into it easier. In late summer or fall, I will often broadfork prior to sowing cover crop seeds. Another benefit of broadforking before winter's freezes is that it allows moisture and snow to work down into the soil; as the water freezes and expands in the soil pockets, it creates better soil aeration. I find that the need for broadforking is virtually eliminated after several years of regenerative practices because the soil becomes naturally aerated and spongy thanks to more active soil life.

REDUCING THE NEED FOR TILLAGE OVER TIME

When you first start regenerative gardening, the process might feel overwhelming. The good news is, as you integrate regenerative practices into your garden, you will also begin to reduce or eliminate the need for tillage and amendments. In effect, you let nature take the lead on managing fertility, pest pressure, organic matter, and the soil food web.

There are other ways we can support nature in creating a complete ecosystem without relying on outside amendments. The next chapter discusses how to "close the garden loop" by using what we have at hand as well as the potential of integrating animals into the regenerative garden.

7

Establish a Closed-Loop Garden

MODERN GARDENS HAVE BECOME INCREDIBLY RELIANT on purchased amendments, such as pesticides, herbicides, fertilizers, bagged soils, and composts. The answer to making the garden more self-sustaining, affordable, and in line with nature's garden lies in upcycling garden waste into homemade amendments and integrating animal inputs within the system where possible to enhance fertility, manage pests, and improve overall ecosystem health. These inputs can include using animals for grazing, supplying manure for compost, and targeting specific garden pests.

Closing the loop in regenerative gardening involves creating a self-sustaining system where resources are recycled within the garden ecosystem. Animals provide natural fertilizers (manure or wool), help soil health through grazing, and aid in pest control by foraging on weeds and garden pests.

This three-bin compost system made of recycled pallets at the farm allows for one pile to be added to, one pile that is cooking, and one that is done and ready for use.

Using Compost in the Garden

When we started our first beds at the farm, I trucked in several loads of high-quality compost (after verifying that it was 100 percent biosolid-free). Not only was the compost costly, but it took backbreaking work to spread and ended up causing my phosphorus and soil salinity levels to shoot through the roof. I am still trying to fix this—phosphorus takes years to come down once levels have spiked. The compost was largely animal-manure based (primarily cow manure). That explains why the phosphorus levels were so high, and this is not uncommon: Animal manure is a primary ingredient of many bulk composts. While manure can help boost microbial activity and provides a good dose of heat-creating nitrogen, it is not always beneficial to include it in compost.

In hindsight, I would have been better off using just a small amount of compost (or making my own at home, though it's unlikely I would have been able to make enough to cover the entire space) and relying more heavily on cover crops to add the organic matter needed to help decompact my soil and create the spongy texture that comes with an active soil food web.

Composting for a Healthy Planet

This is not to say that compost is a bad thing. Composting is certainly good for the planet. Approximately one third of the food produced worldwide ends up in landfills—a massive amount of waste. About 50 percent of the garbage we throw out is compostable (21 percent food waste, 8 percent yard waste, and the remaining wood scraps and paper waste). If more homeowners and gardeners composted their own food scraps and made their own compost, we would cut carbon emissions from landfills equivalent to 1.13 to 1.40 gigatons of carbon dioxide by 2050. This is because as food waste and organic matter break down in the absence of oxygen, they emit methane, a greenhouse gas that traps 25 times more atmospheric heat than CO_2. Therefore, composting is one of the most powerful things we can do as home gardeners both to reduce the climate impact of our organic-matter waste and to aid the health of our gardens.

Homemade compost gives you the advantage of knowing exactly what's in it, unlike commercially made compost, which can contain PFAS, persistent herbicides, microplastics, and excessive phosphorus and salts (see page 56).

So while composting is a good thing to do for both our gardens and our planet, compost should be considered an amendment to the soil, not a growing medium. It is excellent when applied in moderation to add small amounts of organic matter and, primarily, active soil microbes. This is why homemade will always trump store-bought composts: Not only will homemade compost contain native microbes that are local to your area, but it will have more soil life present within it than a bag of compost that has been sitting (especially in the hot sun). If you can't make it at home, source a locally made compost, preferably OMRI certified.

A Basic Guide to Home Composting

When first starting a compost pile, it is easy to worry about every input, as well as ratios, turning, and precise temperatures. This can quickly become overwhelming, and when we become overwhelmed, we are less likely to try new things. So instead of detailing all the various methods of composting (and there are many, including Bokashi composting, cold and hot composting, Johnson-Su bioreactor composting, and more), we will keep it simple here.

How to Start a Compost Pile

Most of us busy home gardeners simply don't have the time or energy to expend a lot of thought or effort on our compost piles—and the good news is, you don't have to. While certain methods can provide a technically better-quality compost with higher levels of certain microbes and at a faster speed, you will achieve perfectly good compost (albeit one that takes slightly longer to mature) with a more hands-off approach.

Find bins. Here at the farm, I use a three-bin system made of recycled, untreated wooden pallets (we simply connected intact pallets to form a back wall and dividers). The bins are closed on three sides and open on the front, which makes turning and digging easier. We have one bin that is finished (or nearly finished), one that is actively composting, and one that we are actively adding to. If you don't have space for pallet bins, look into collapsible composting bins that can be expanded as you fill them and have open holes on the sides for airflow, which I much prefer to enclosed tumblers—those tend to get very hot and dry out materials quickly. Recycled or reused materials are always preferable to purchased, though, so seek out materials you can give a second life to whenever possible.

Layer leaves. I start the bottom of the pile by cutting back any existing vegetation and layering 8 to 12 inches of leaves on the bottom. This will not only smother any weeds or grasses (except, of course, for aggressive rhizome-based grasses like Bermuda), but it will also provide some fungi and heat to get your compost pile started. Leaves, too, offer a bit of aeration from the bottom of the pile, which will help your compost cook a bit faster.

I added a thick layer of browns in the form of shredded leaves to start the compost pile.

Starting a compost pile with a thick layer of leaves (above left) followed by garden greens and food scraps (above right), a shovelful of garden soil, and more browns (opposite top left) helps reach a balance to promote the most microbially active compost (far right).

Add organic matter. Now you can begin adding your materials. A healthy compost pile will contain a mixture of brown and green materials. Browns are carbon-rich materials such as leaves, dried grass clippings, dry yard waste, and straw/wood shavings used as animal bedding (which can be considered a green if they contain a lot of manure). Greens are nitrogen-rich materials like food scraps, fresh green grass clippings, weeds and yard waste, coffee grounds, and manure (more on that in a bit).

Layer greens and browns. On top of your base browns layer, add your first layer of greens. Each time you add a pile of greens, you'll want to top that with about two to three times that amount in browns such as leaves. The smaller the layering materials are chopped, the faster the composting process will be. Continue to layer browns and greens until the pile is about 4 feet high, and then let it begin the cooking process.

Toss in some soil. Take a shovelful of soil from a neighbor's healthy compost pile, underneath some healthy perennials, or from an existing space where healthy vegetation is growing, and sprinkle it in as you build your layers. This will jump-start the pile by bringing in some members of your native soil food web.

Let it sit. Often, by the time you've added enough materials to reach the top of your compost pile (I like to build it about 4 feet tall), the layers on the bottom have already begun to compost. You can opt to turn the compost at this point or to simply let it sit. Whether you turn your compost or not is a matter of personal choice; both methods have their pros and cons. Be sure to keep the materials moist, adding water as needed.

Build a Leaf Tower

It can be difficult to have enough browns on hand at all times, so we construct simple leaf towers made of rabbit fencing—a wire fencing with narrower openings on the bottom and wider ones on top. (Rabbit fencing can also be handy to have around if you battle bunnies in the garden!)

Cut long pieces of rabbit fencing, shape them into rounds, and loop the cut ends together to form a bin shape. In fall, we gather up as many leaves as possible and put them in the towers; this not only helps keep them from blowing off the property (and making the neighbors angry), but it also provides protected habitat for leaf-nesting insects over the winter. As you need browns for your compost, simply grab a handful from your leaf tower and toss it into your compost pile.

Hot Versus Cold Composting

I typically like hot composting, as it helps ensure any pathogens in the animal manure produced here at the farm aren't spread around my garden. It also yields finished results faster than cold composting. But cold composting is a legitimate method, too, especially for those of us who are busy doing things other than turning compost!

HOT COMPOSTING

To keep your compost hot and "cooking" faster, you'll want to turn it more frequently and water it occasionally (keep it moist, not dried out or soggy). Turning more frequently will not only result in compost more quickly, it will also help kill pathogens, so it can be a good idea to hot compost if your green materials contain weed seeds or manure. However, hot composting requires more time to maintain—something home gardeners can be in short supply of.

To keep the compost at the temperatures required to kill pathogens and weed seeds, grab a compost thermometer. Once you build your pile, you'll want it to reach the ideal temperature of 141 to 160°F (61 to 71°C) and maintain that temperature for several days to a week or longer. If the temperature drops to 140°F (60°C) or below, or if it gets hotter than 160°F (71°C), turn the pile again and add water. Repeat this process several times. A hot pile takes more effort but will produce compost in several weeks to several months, and it will have a greater volume than a cold compost because it's being turned.

COLD COMPOSTING

Cold composting, on the other hand, doesn't require any turning of the pile, making for a slower composting process but one that demands much less effort. You'll start out the same way as hot composting: creating the compost pile by layering greens and browns. But then you let a cold compost pile simply sit so that nature does the work. It can take months or up to two years, depending on air temperatures, for cold compost to reach a completed stage. To speed up the cold composting process, chop up your browns and

This compost is nearly finished but still contains some large chunks; sifting will remove any larger pieces if needed.

greens into smaller pieces that will break down significantly faster.

Gardeners who cold compost should not include weeds that have gone to seed or plants with diseases like powdery mildew, as temperatures won't reach high enough to kill them. Cold composting can also contribute more methane, a greenhouse gas, to the atmosphere, because it leads to decomposition in the absence of oxygen. If you want to minimize your carbon footprint, cold composting might not be for you.

Either method, cold or hot, will provide you with excellent compost to use in your garden, but at different speeds and with varying levels of effort required. The process can be as simple or as complicated as you want—either way, the goal is to get started making your own compost and closing the waste loop in your garden!

What Not to Add to the Compost Pile

Some composting styles allow you to compost almost anything. With Bokashi, for example, you add to your scraps in a bucket a wheat bran/microbial amendment called bokashi flakes and let it break down in the absence of oxygen—an excellent composting method if you have limited indoor or outdoor space. But it is generally best to avoid feces (human, canine, and feline), animal bones and scraps, and dairy products in home compost piles. Not only can they contain dangerous pathogens, they can also attract a lot of rodents while they break down.

Animal by-products, bones, and dairy can be composted in municipal facilities with large piles that are constantly turned and that heat up for long periods, but this is more difficult to manage on a home scale. Some paper products can be composted, but we prefer not to due to the concerns about chemicals used to bleach paper products and the release of dioxins, PFAS, and other chemicals in compostable paper products. We put those in a recycling bin instead.

If you want to speed up your compost pile (whether using the hot or cold method), mix up a batch of alfalfa fertilizer (see page 190) and add it to the center of your pile; this will create heat and get things moving.

How to Deal with Rodents

Yes, it's absolutely possible that your compost pile will attract rodents. While we believe mice and rats can be a key part of an ecosystem (after all, they are food for hawks, owls, and foxes, which also help keep rabbit populations in check), there can be too many.

- To discourage rodents and other animals from nesting in the pile, turn your compost more frequently to speed decomposition.
- Bury a layer of hardware mesh under your compost pile and around the sides to help minimize nibblers.
- If this doesn't help, a compost tumbler may be the right option for you—but be sure to moisten the contents often, as they tend to dry out rapidly in that hot and elevated environment. A tumbler may also contribute microplastics to your compost due to the heat and moisture within—important to note if you are avoiding plastics in the garden.
- Electric tabletop composters, while expensive, are another good alternative if you live on a city lot or don't have much space to compost. They require electricity to run, but this usage is offset by the amount of methane saved by not landfilling compostable materials. They are typically made of plastic and generate carbon emissions during manufacture, however, so only consider them if other rodent mitigation options don't work.
- Alternatively, seek out a municipal compost program. Some such programs give participants the option to purchase back compost. Be sure to properly vet the other components of municipal composts and ensure that biosolids are not being added. If they are, I recommend avoiding them.

Animal Integration

Animal integration and grazing are key elements in regenerative agriculture. Animals close the garden loop by replenishing the soil. They harvest the energy converted from sunlight by plants and turn it into valuable fuel and fertility for the garden. Allowing a ruminant animal, such as a sheep or cow, to eat and trample down your cover crop at the end of its growing cycle, and leaving the nutrient-rich manure in place, will return nutrients directly to the soil and improve its health. And you don't necessarily need large animals—these same benefits can be achieved fairly easily with smaller creatures such as bunnies, chickens, small sheep, or goats.

Domestic animals provide a closed loop of nutrient cycling and the best benefits, which is why the ideal integration scenario is for animals to physically live on (or visit) your property. But what about for the home gardener? For many smaller-scale urban or suburban home lots, that isn't always an option. Your neighborhood or lot may not be zoned for animals. Maybe your garden is on a balcony. Or perhaps you don't have the time or desire to maintain animals on a property—and that is okay, too! You can still adopt the principle of a closed-loop garden in other ways, such as through worm farming or by adding locally sourced manures to composts or garden amendment recipes to gain the benefits of manure's microbial life and nitrogen content.

Roosevelt and Midnight, the Southdown Babydoll sheep at the farm, graze a cover crop.

One of the farm's chickens roams in some mature landscaping, perusing for earwigs under mulch layers.

Is Animal Integration Right for Your Garden?

Although animals can make an excellent addition to the regenerative garden, the decision to bring them in should not be made without serious consideration. Animals, after all, are a commitment and can be a costly one at that!

THE BENEFITS OF ANIMALS IN THE GARDEN

Of course, having animals is useful if you want to supplement your family's diet with fresh eggs, dairy, or even meat. But here are a few ways that having animals incorporated into our garden space helps our goals in the regenerative garden.

Soil health. The first benefit is obviously to the soil. Regenerative agriculture tries to emulate the effect that herds of grazing bison had on building the dense soil of the midwestern prairies by bringing in animals to eat the top part of grass, deposit nutrient-rich manure, trample it in, and then move to another area before they have overgrazed any one location. The benefits of on-site animal manure and urine to the microbial load of the soil are unmistakable and are the fastest way to bring depleted soil back to good health.

Composting. Our chickens scratch through our compost pile, which helps to turn it, and they nourish themselves by eating bugs and scraps, which reduces our feed costs. Chicken manure is also nitrogen rich and thus helps heat up our compost pile; it serves as a kick-starter in new piles or reinvigorates a pile that has cooled off prematurely.

After I clean out the sheep pen, the mix of manure and bedding goes into the compost pile to create a rich garden amendment full of microbial activity.

Midnight and Roosevelt graze a cover-cropped row within an electric fence to keep them from eating valuable dahlias.

Incorporation of manure/compost. After our sheep come through the areas of the garden we want them to graze, we send the chickens in to scratch the manure into the soil as they search for grubs and bugs.

Weed and invasive species control. Animals such as goats can be incredibly helpful in the removal and control of invasive species, particularly if you are trying to clear or rewild larger spaces. If we pen the animals into a smaller area, they will quickly clear most vegetation, which can be helpful in preparing a new garden site. Unfortunately, it can also mean they may eat some of the plants you are trying to keep!

While some plants are toxic for animals to eat, a good many weeds can be eaten by livestock and turned into fertilizer via the animal digestive system. I was thrilled to find my sheep seeking out and chowing down on the bindweed in our field while completely ignoring my lavender. However, this is not to say that they won't chomp into my pumpkins or dahlias if given the opportunity, so we've learned to be cautious and not allow access to certain plants. And when we pull large weeds or unwanted plants in the garden, we toss them to the sheep to convert to nutrient-rich manure that we can add to the compost pile.

A few words of caution here: If you are not hot composting your animal manure, try to avoid allowing your animals to eat weed seeds, which pass through their systems and can still be viable in their manure. Also be sure you aren't feeding your animals anything that might be toxic, such as milkweed or sweet peas. Check with your state extension service to determine which plants in your area are poisonous to livestock.

Pest control. Chickens, guinea hens, and ducks are excellent at controlling pests like grubs, slugs, grasshoppers, ticks, and more. We've seen chickens run and fight over grasshoppers in the summer garden, which is not only amusing but so satisfying!

Terminating cover crops. Our sheep do their best work when it comes to terminating cover crops. By grazing in the garden after the cover crop is done growing, they directly help improve the soil by trampling and breaking down plants and leaving deposits of microbe-rich urine and manure. I'm always sure to select cover crops that are safe for grazing animals.

CHALLENGES WITH ANIMALS IN THE GARDEN

While we love having our animals on-site, it isn't always fun—they come with a lot of responsibility and effort. Here are some of the downsides.

Space limitations. While we are on approximately 2 acres, about one third of that is dedicated to wildlife habitat and some to our home, so the area we have for animals is limited. This can make rotating them and giving them sufficient space a challenge.

Zoning rules. If you live in an urban or suburban area, there's a good chance zoning will limit what kinds of animals, and how many, you are allowed to keep on your property. Be sure to check into this before you invest in animals and infrastructure. It's also a good idea to inform neighbors of your plans and discuss any of their concerns together before bringing animals to your space.

Shelter. Animals need some sort of protection from extreme weather. Although our sheep are happy with a basic structure that shelters them from wind and rain (ours is a three-sided lean-to), our chickens require a much more secure environment to prevent predation. We kept costs down by using reclaimed and reused materials, but building and maintaining shelters takes money and time. You also need to check local zoning requirements to see if your structure requires a permit.

Maintenance. Some animals are lower maintenance than others. Our chickens require only an hour or so of dedicated time each week to maintain their coop, feed and water them, and gather eggs. The sheep, on the other hand, require more effort: annual shearing, hoof trimming every few months, daily water changes, and cheek scratches every now and then! We also rotate their grazing area using portable electric fencing with a solar charger to keep them from overgrazing a site and to minimize the risks of intestinal worms and parasites, which can be more common when animals are kept in one area for too long. While this maintenance is

This makeshift chicken coop was fashioned from an old play structure that I found for free in a neighborhood group. I wrapped it in hardware cloth to make it predator proof.

The sheep pen is outfitted with an electric wire to keep out predators; the sheep require only a simple lean-to style structure for protection from the elements.

Sheep can be escape artists, but they are also good at break-ins—they love to come into the workshop on hot summer days, where they've been known to eat buckets of dahlias and roses!

simpler in real life than it sounds, it can also be too much work for most home gardeners. Be mindful of your reality, property size, and whether animals fit into your schedule.

Cost. We graze our animals in the warmer months, but winter requires us to buy supplemental food, which can get costly. Veterinary bills also come up, just as with any animal, and the expense of large-animal vet visits can add up quickly!

Predation. Chickens are extremely vulnerable to predation, regardless of where you live. Even urban areas have foxes, owls, and others creatures that will happily eat a chicken or go after their eggs. Hawks and owls can swoop in from above, racoons and bobcats can climb over fences, and other animals can burrow underground to get at your birds, so protect your fowl on all four sides by enclosing the coop and run with ¼-inch hardware mesh. Planning ahead to avoid predation can help, but there are always unexpected attacks. I've had coyotes enter my farm during the middle of the day and pick off chickens less than 100 feet away from me, and it can be heartbreaking if they are pets. Offer as much protection as you can, and always exercise caution. Larger animals like sheep can benefit from electric fencing and motion-activated lights or sprinklers to help keep larger predators out.

Eating wanted plants and garden damage. Animals can sometimes get into areas we don't want them to be in and do some damage! Chickens can eat and destroy new plantings in spring, sheep can munch roses and tree bark, and goats will devour everything in sight (including the siding on your house). So bear in mind that to protect your garden, you must have fencing plans in place, whether they are permanent or movable electric fences to contain your fluffy and feathered friends! As previously noted, certain plants can be toxic for grazing animals, including milkweed, sweet peas, chokecherries, and yarrow. While our sheep naturally avoid these plants if they have other food to eat, it is wise to be mindful of which plants you must exclude.

Compaction. If your space isn't big enough to continually rotate larger animals like goats and

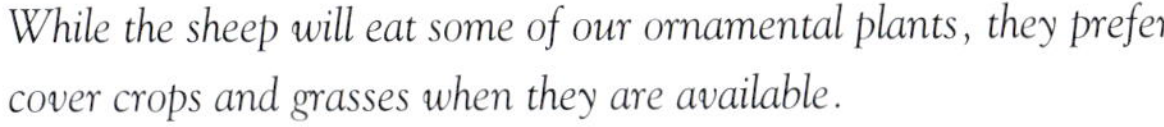

While the sheep will eat some of our ornamental plants, they prefer cover crops and grasses when they are available.

In this wild meadow area, we don't allow the sheep to graze because we don't want them to eat the pollinator plants or the toxic milkweed.

sheep, soil compaction can occur from them constantly trampling the ground and eating vegetation.

Disruption of the native ecosystem. If regeneration of native plants is a major motivation for your garden, animals (grazing ones in particular) can sometimes be harmful. For example, our sheep can be detrimental in areas we are trying to rewild with native grasses, as the sheep relish some native grasses, like little bluestem, when they are small. Goats, in particular, are not choosy about what they eat and can be majorly destructive in the landscape.

Potential pathogens. Pathogens can be spread when fresh animal manure is used on edible produce (particularly in the case of carnivorous animals, which is why we don't use dog or cat feces in compost). This is why aging or hot composting manure is advised.

There are many benefits of having animals in the regenerative garden but several downsides as well. Consider your needs and these

Chickens are lighter and therefore don't cause the compaction that heavier animals can.

possibilities carefully; the last thing you want is to bring home animals you are not prepared for and thus need to rehome later.

ETHICAL CONSIDERATIONS

Additionally, there are ethical considerations when bringing animals into the garden. How long will the animals be with you—and what are your plans for them in the long term? Will you be raising these animals for meat consumption, or will they be lifelong pets? What will happen to your chickens at the end of their egg-producing life? If raising them for meat consumption, will you be butchering them yourself or hiring someone?

These are very personal decisions that only you can make. Here at the farm, we've chosen to raise our chickens and sheep as pets, and they will live out their lives here, which is quite a commitment (sheep live 12 to 14 years)! But there are many gardeners and backyard homesteaders who decide to raise their chickens for meat and enjoy knowing where their food is coming from and how it was raised. It is a personal decision in which the quality of life and respect for the animal need to be strongly considered.

Small Animals

It's always been my dream to have a milk cow—to walk outside and get fresh milk, make my own butter and cheese, graze a cow on a wide-open expanse of pasture, and know that the animal I'm sourcing from is in good health and well cared for. Alas, it is not possible (or humane) on a small lot with a large space dedicated to gardens and habitat, so I shall have to wait to fulfill my homemade butter dreams. However, there are a number of smaller animal options for suburban lots that can be beneficial in the regenerative garden—but each comes with its own set of pros and cons to weigh carefully.

Rabbits. These make an adorable addition to the small backyard garden and double as fluffy pets while also providing excellent fertilizer. Rabbits require enclosed hutches, as they are quite vulnerable to predation, as well as

Pet rabbits are both adorable and useful, as they contribute fertilizer to the garden. They can be vulnerable to predation and require secure shelters.

requiring significant additional living space to exercise and explore. Their manure is the easiest to gather and add to the garden, because it is in a dry pellet form and does not require aging before being applied. While we don't keep rabbits at the farm, we do have a great many in our backyard, and we regularly collect their poop to place directly into planting holes in spring. Rabbit manure has an N-P-K (nitrogen-phosphorus-potassium) ratio of approximately 2.4–1.4–0.6.

Chickens. It's rewarding to raise chickens as part of the backyard garden, particularly if you enjoy eggs! Not only can chickens make fun pets with lots of personality, they can also provide beneficial nitrogen in the form of manure to add to compost piles and, eventually, the garden. And they are excellent at grub control and snacking on other pests such as earwigs and grasshoppers. Unfortunately, they can be destructive in the garden, scratching through soil and bathing in the dirt, so be careful releasing them into the garden in spring, when they can damage small seedlings.

Backyard birds require a very safe enclosure (see page 175), especially for the dusk-to-dawn hours, as they are a favorite meal among predators such as foxes, even in urban spaces. While they can be somewhat smelly in larger numbers (especially in summer heat!), using layers of pine shavings and keeping a clean coop will help keep the odor at bay. Chicken manure requires additional aging before being used directly in the garden. Its N-P-K ratio is around 1.1–0.8–0.5.

Ducks. These are excellent at controlling pests like slugs, mosquito larvae, grubs, snails, grasshoppers, and more—and they aren't as destructive as chickens, because they don't tend to dig. Duck eggs are very nutritious. These birds need a protective enclosure like chickens, and most breeds also need access to water. If you don't have a pond, a kiddie pool will do, but the water needs to be changed frequently.

Duck manure can be used directly in the garden without composting, but it is somewhat liquid and can be a bit challenging to gather. The N-P-K ratio is around 2.8–2.3–1.7.

Goats and sheep. I'd been wanting sheep on the farm for a long time, and two years ago we finally got Midnight and Roosevelt, our two Babydoll Southdown sheep. Even though sheep and goats are the smaller of the ruminant animals, they are still on the larger side for urban and suburban lots and can be challenging to keep, though they come with some excellent benefits, too! Many cities allow these animals, provided the lot is large enough.

Goats and sheep graze down weeds and unwanted vegetation. Goats are great for shrubby plants and lots of weeds, while sheep are the lawnmowers of the ruminant world, neatly shearing grass down without pulling the roots out. If you want an indiscriminate eater, go with goats; sheep are pickier eaters and aren't as agile as goats, tending to keep all four feet on the ground and graze grasses rather than trees and shrubs. Both animals will escape if given the opportunity, so they need safe and strong enclosures to prevent them from pushing out and getting into trouble.

This chicken, Dottie, loves to scratch through the mulch in the lavender field.

We use our sheep to graze down our cover crops as well as grassy areas of the farm, containing them with portable electric fencing on a solar charger, which can be moved quickly and easily. They are wonderful pets (they recognize our faces and come when called), and we use their wool for felt crafting, making wool dryer balls, and milling into yarn. We also use it in the garden as soil mulch and in seed starting. Wool is a slow-release source of nitrogen and is excellent at retaining moisture (see page 180).

Using Wool in the Garden

Sheep require annual shearing or their wool can become too heavy and even kill them. Wool is a natural by-product of sheep farming, but much shorn wool gets discarded as "seconds" because it is too short or dirty for use in textiles.

When we brought Midnight and Roosevelt to the farm, I intended to spin their wool into yarn. In reality, I was never going to have time to do this, and bags of wool started piling up in my shed. On a whim one day as I was filling my wood trays for seed starting, I thought I'd throw some wool in the bottom to help keep the soil in place and provide moisture retention. Those plants grew faster and were thicker, healthier, and a darker green than the counterparts I sowed without the wool—and every following trial showed the same results.

I started using wool in my planting holes and as a garden mulch. While my two sheep don't provide sufficient wool to mulch my entire field, they produce enough for me to drop a bit of wool in nearly every planting hole.

There are myriad benefits of wool in the garden beyond its sustainability as a renewable resource. It can be used for:

- **Soil improvement.** Wool contains slow-release nitrogen (with an N-P-K of around 9-0-2). As it breaks down, it also helps to aerate the soil and improve drainage.
- **Pest control.** Wool used as a mulch or barrier is a natural deterrent for certain garden pests, such as slugs, due to its rough texture.
- **Mulching.** Wool shredded or chopped into small pieces and used as a mulch will help with moisture retention and soil temperature regulation.

I now use wool throughout the garden: in the bottoms of containers and pots, in planting holes, as a mulch, and in seed starting. If you can, source raw wool from a local farmer whom you trust to treat their animals humanely.

Earthworms consume decaying material and microbes, contributing to a healthy soil system.

The need for annual shearing does add some cost to keeping sheep. Other routine maintenance includes hoof trimming every few months and regular veterinary care for vaccinations and issues like intestinal parasites. Their manure is small, dry, and pelleted, which makes it easy to collect and much less odorous than horse or cow manure. Sheep and goat manure's N-P-K ratio is around 0.7–0.3–0.9.

While animals may seem like a cute and fun way to incorporate regenerative practices into a larger garden (and they certainly can be!), remember that caution must be taken with phosphorus levels and that animals require a great deal of commitment and effort to be cared for ethically. Think the decision through carefully. If you decide animals aren't a good fit for your space, a good alternative can be to seek out animal-owning friends who won't mind contributing to your compost pile, and there are several simple soil amendments that can be good substitutes for animal manure as well.

Earthworms in the Regenerative Garden

Don't have room for animals (or a compost pile)? A lot of us home gardeners don't! Luckily there's an alternative: Have you ever considered becoming a worm farmer? If not, you may want to. Not only will it help you in the composting process, it can save you money—especially if you're using our seed-starting recipe with worm castings. It's a great way to close the garden loop by turning your garden and kitchen scraps into soil you can use to start seed.

Worm composting, also known as vermiculture, is an eco-friendly way to recycle organic waste and create nutrient-rich fertilizer for your garden. I consider worms to be an "animal input" in the realm of regenerative gardening and farming, as they are living organisms. They contribute to soil fertility by digesting waste and converting it into a highly bioavailable form of nutrients for plants.

STARTING A WORM BIN

Creating a worm bin is simple, and it's easy to tailor your bin to your available space. Here's how to get started.

Choose a container: Use a wooden bin with a lid to avoid contributing microplastics; cedar is ideal for drainage. Ensure the bin has ventilation holes for airflow and drainage holes to prevent bedding and worms from getting waterlogged.

Select the right worms: Red wigglers are the most common worms for composting. They thrive in organic material and are efficient at breaking it down. That said, they can also be invasive, so if you select them, I recommend keeping your worm bin separate from your garden space to prevent escapees. Alternatively, simply dig up as many worms as you can from your garden and landscape to start your worm bin.

Prepare bedding: Worm bedding mimics the worms' natural habitat and provides them with a comfortable environment. My preferred bedding includes a mix of coconut coir, aged leaves, and straw, along with a scoop of garden soil or finished compost to introduce beneficial microbes. Moisten the bedding until damp, like a wrung-out sponge.

Feeding and maintaining the worms: Worms can eat the same things that go in your compost pile: fruit and vegetable scraps, coffee grounds, eggshells, and other organic waste (try to add everything in moderation). As with our outdoor compost pile, I avoid adding meat, dairy, and citrus—these can harm the worms and attract pests.

Layer the food: Bury food scraps in different sections of the bin to avoid odors and pests, starting with about 3 to 5 parts food scraps to 1 part bedding so it doesn't overheat.

Conditions: Keep the bin in a cool, shaded area, ideally between 55 and 77°F (13 to 25°C). This may mean bringing the bin into a garage over winter or in the heat of summer. Worms are sensitive to extreme heat, cold, and direct sunlight.

Harvesting worm castings: After a few months, the worms will have converted most of the bedding and food into dark, crumbly castings suitable for seed starting. To harvest, you can try one of the following methods.

- Migration: Push the finished compost to one side of the bin and add fresh bedding and food to the other side. The worms will migrate to the new food, allowing you to scoop out castings.
- Light separation: Dump the contents onto a tarp and form small mounds. Worms will burrow down away from the light, letting you collect the castings from the top part of the mounds.
- Sifting: Use a sifter with ¼- to ⅛-inch openings. Dry the castings out slightly, gather them, and start with a small amount in the sifter. Gently shake it back and forth over a container or tarp, and place the remaining worms or undigested pieces of food into a new bin with fresh bedding.

Store castings in a cool, dark place to preserve the beneficial microbes.

NO NEED TO BUY EARTHWORMS

While a worm bin can help you compost food scraps and minimize the need for purchasing soil for seed starting or amending containers, purchasing worms to add to your garden beds is typically unnecessary. Some purchased worms, such as the red wigglers, can actually harm North American ecosystems, as they can escape and invade woodlands, where they can do significant damage. Simply practicing the recommendations prescribed in this book will bring you plenty of earthworms to wrangle: Limit soil disturbance, provide mulch as a cover, and leave living roots in the ground as much as possible. Earthworms provide an excellent example of how the system will work for you if you let nature take the lead in the garden.

Closing the Nutrient Loop: Soil Amendment Recipes

A healthy and functioning soil that incorporates organic-matter mulching, cover cropping for living roots, and minimal disturbance will facilitate ecosystem health and help soil microbes mineralize soil nutrients. However, amendments can speed the process, which is especially helpful when beginning your regenerative gardening journey.

The following amendment recipes don't require many outside inputs and won't increase nutrient levels to a point that could negatively impact the balance of your soil. These recipes are mostly focused on increasing soil life but can also help add nitrogen. If any of these recipes seem overwhelming to you, remember that they are *not* required. Following the other principles in this book, especially cover cropping and mulching with organic matter, will provide your soil with nutrients and the environment for the soil life to thrive and become a regenerative system.

Track the success or effects of these recipes to determine whether they seem helpful in your garden. Side-by-side comparisons can provide considerable insight.

Several of these recipes can utilize animal manure or other animal inputs as ingredients. While keeping animals on-site allows you control over their feed and living conditions, there are other ways to obtain their positive effects on your garden's soil health and soil food web. Local small farms will often give away or sell small amounts of manure that can be added directly to your compost pile and used in the following recipes. Age the manure for three to four months before using to minimize any pathogen risks. If you cannot source manure, worm castings can be used. Homemade compost will provide excellent benefits in these recipes in the form of microbial biomass, but it will not provide much nitrogen. You can supplement nitrogen with an alfalfa fertilizer, a nitrogen-fixing cover crop, or wool pellets.

On the Topic of Macronutrients

Why do I omit a recipe for phosphorus and potassium supplementation?

Most fertilizers do more harm than good or are simply unnecessary. It is far too easy to over-amend our soils with nutrients, and some nutrients, such as phosphorus, negatively affect both garden performance and ecosystem health. Excess phosphorus has been shown to reduce mycorrhizal populations in soil, but the presence of mycorrhizae in the soil is key to a plant's ability to take up existing phosphorus. Potassium and phosphorus are supplied naturally via the weathering of rocks degraded by microbes and plants such as lichen, which creates a flow of minerals to plants via mycorrhizal fungi. Instead of adding potassium and phosphorus to soil and crossing our fingers, we can focus on nurturing our soil life. If, however, your soil phosphorus and potassium levels are very low, consult your state extension service for organic recommendations.

COMPOST SLURRY DIP FOR PLANTING

Makes one gallon slurry dip

This is one of the simplest ways I have found to inoculate plant roots with native microbes. It serves two purposes: First, it gets the microbes right up next to the plant roots; and second, it ensures the seedlings are thoroughly moist at planting time, which helps minimize transplant shock. The molasses feeds and encourages bacteria to multiply, which aids in the rhizophagy process. If you can, source raw wool or wool pellets to place at the bottom of each hole before planting, to provide slow-release nitrogen and moisture retention.

MATERIALS

- 1-gallon bucket filled with rainwater or dechlorinated tap water (let tap water sit for 24 to 36 hours in an open container to dechlorinate)
- 1 cup homemade compost
- 1 tablespoon unsulfured molasses
- Raw wool or wool pellets (optional)

Mix the water, compost, and molasses together and let sit for a couple of hours and up to overnight in a shady location. At planting time, place a rootball into the dip and let the liquid saturate the roots before placing the rootball in the ground. Add a tablespoon of wool pellets or a 2-inch piece of raw wool in the bottom of the planting hole, if desired, for additional slow-release nitrogen.

Adding molasses to dechlorinated water helps inoculants work more effectively.

Stir in the compost and molasses and let it sit for a couple of hours and up to overnight in a shady location prior to using.

WEED TEA

Makes 3–4 gallons
weed tea concentrate

If your soil test indicates mineral deficiencies, weed tea is a great solution. Not only does it add trace nutrients, it also utilizes a free resource—weeds! Weeds, especially taproot weeds like dandelions, common mallow, and burdock, extract minerals from deep within the ground that can then be extracted in this tea. Apply to plants and soil during the growing season at dusk.

MATERIALS

- 4–5 gallons rainwater or dechlorinated tap water (let tap water sit for 24 to 36 hours in an open container to dechlorinate)
- 5-gallon bucket filled to the top with taproot weeds (get a diverse mix!)
- Bubbler aerator
- Heavy stone or brick
- Grain bag or cheesecloth

Pour in enough of the water to fill the 5-gallon bucket of weeds to the top. Place the end of the aerator into the bottom of the bucket and turn it on. Set a heavy stone or brick on top of the weeds to weigh them down below the water level. Plug in the aerator and leave the bucket in a partially shaded area for 3 to 4 weeks.

Strain the weeds (they can go in your compost pile if you are hot composting) through the grain bag. If weed seeds are present, strain through a cheesecloth to avoid adding them to your beds. To use, dilute at a ratio of 1 part weed tea to 10 parts water before applying to plants and soil at dusk.

Cover weeds in a bucket with water.

Add an aerator to the bucket.

Use a rock to weigh down and submerge weeds.

After aging, strain out the weeds and dilute the tea to use on plants.

COMPOST TEA

Makes 5 gallons compost tea concentrate

Compost tea can be used as an alternative to fungicides in the garden. It's ideally made with homemade compost, which contains the microbes native to your area that will survive the best in your garden. Or you can use soil from healthy garden beds or from around plants in your garden to multiply microbes in compost. Start the process in the evening so the tea will be ready to apply around dusk the following day.

Place compost into a grain bag or cheesecloth and tie a knot in the top.

Place the compost bag into a 5-gallon bucket.

Add an aerator. Weight it if needed to hold it down at the bottom of the bucket.

MATERIALS

- 2 cups high-quality homemade compost or soil from a healthy garden spot
- Grain bag or cheesecloth
- 5-gallon bucket filled with rainwater or dechlorinated tap water (let tap water sit for 24 to 36 hours in an open container to dechlorinate)
- Bubbler aerator
- Heavy rock or brick

Place the compost in the grain bag and tie it up. Set the bag into the bucket of water, insert the aerator, and weight the aerator with a heavy rock or brick so it stays at the bottom of the bucket.

Let the compost tea steep for approximately 24 hours. To use, dilute it at a ratio of 1 part compost tea to 4 parts water, and apply to the soil at dusk.

Dilute the tea with dechlorinated water before using.

Apply to soil at dusk.

LEAF MOLD

Yield: Finished product will yield approximately 20% of starting quantity

This leaf mold can be used in potting mixes, as a soil amendment to add organic matter, or as a substitute for the compost in the compost tea recipe (page 186). It is simple to make but requires patience!

It works best to use mulched (chopped) leaves instead of whole, but since many pollinators nest within leaves, we pile them up in fall and mulch them in spring after temperatures are consistently above 50°F (10°C) to give eggs and nesting pollinators time to emerge.

Fill a large bin with leaves. Mulched leaves will finish faster than whole leaves.

Add a living soil, such as that from your garden or compost from your compost bin.

Wet the mix to the consistency of a wrung-out sponge.

MATERIALS

- Leaves (mulched or whole)
- Large metal trash can with a lid
- Handful of good garden soil or compost
- Rain water or dechlorinated tap water (let tap water sit for 24 to 36 hours in an open container to dechlorinate)

Put the leaves into the trash can, add the soil, and pour in some dechlorinated tap water or rainwater until the leaves are moist. Place the lid on the can and let it sit in a sunny area for 1 to 2 years. (Shake or turn it and add water to keep it moist and speed up the process.) Check every once in a while—the leaf mold is done when its consistency is soil-like.

Cover and place in a sunny spot. Shaking and adding water occasionally will help speed up the process.

The final product is loamy and makes an excellent organic matter amendment for clayey or sandy soil.

ALFALFA FERTILIZER

Makes enough for one 4 × 8-foot bed

This is my go-to recipe for amending containers, raised beds, or newly started in-ground beds in need of some nutrients and organic matter. Not only is this recipe affordable, it's mild. Alfalfa has an N-P-K of 2.5–0.5–2.5, so it's low in phosphorus, which is important for those of us with a history of high phosphorus in our garden soil from too much compost. While it can be a good idea to get a soil test every few years to keep an eye on nutrient levels, you can apply this fertilizer without too much worry. This recipe is adapted from the Rodale Institute.

Alfalfa contains a natural growth hormone called triacontanol, which can improve plant growth and flavor. I buy 40-pound bags of organic alfalfa pellets for around $40 (it's best to source organic, because conventional alfalfa commonly has high rates of herbicide contamination). Add a scoop of homemade compost or native garden soil from around existing plants, pour in some molasses to feed that soil life with carbohydrates, and ferment the mixture for a day before applying to soil.

Add alfalfa pellets to a tub that's large enough to hold water as well.

Add compost from your compost pile or quality soil from a healthy spot of your garden.

Mix molasses and water.

MATERIALS

- 4 pounds organic alfalfa pellets
- Large tub or bin with a lid (or towels large enough to cover the top)
- Scoop of homemade compost or home garden soil
- Large bucket
- 2 tablespoons unsulfured molasses
- 3 quarts lukewarm rainwater or dechlorinated tap water (let tap water sit for 24 to 36 hours in an open container to dechlorinate)

Pour the alfalfa pellets into the tub. Add the compost and stir to combine. Combine the molasses and water in a large bucket and stir to dissolve. Pour the molasses mixture over the alfalfa mixture and stir to moisten.

Cover the tub with a lid or towels and let it sit in a shaded location at room temperature for about 24 hours, stirring every several hours. To use, apply the mixture to soil and gently cultivate it into the top couple of inches just before planting. Alternatively, mix a couple of spoonfuls directly into each planting hole.

Pour the molasses and water mixture over the alfalfa mixture.

Cover with a towel and let it sit in a warm area out of direct sun for 24 hours, stirring occasionally.

Apply to soil before planting or directly into planting holes to get the most out of the fertilizer.

8 Embrace and Observe the Wisdom of Nature

THIS MAY BE THE MOST IMPORTANT CONCEPT YOU TAKE AWAY FROM THIS BOOK: Regenerative gardening requires a fundamental change in mindset. Rather than try to control every problem in the garden and fix them using artificial means, we turn to nature as a guide and a resource for answers. The garden does not operate outside of the ecosystem, but as a part of it.

By observing and emulating the wisdom of natural systems, we can create spaces that thrive in harmony with their environments. This is where the true beauty of regenerative gardening lies: not in achieving flawlessness, but in embracing imperfection and celebrating the diversity of life within our gardens. This is a mindset that encourages us to embrace the messiness of life and to celebrate the diversity of species that call our gardens home. To find beauty in the intricate interplay of growth and decay.

Keep a Garden Journal

The practice of journaling is a powerful tool for deepening our connection to the garden. Wandering through our gardens, notebook in hand, we have the opportunity to slow down, to observe with intention, and to reflect on the lessons that nature has to offer. Whether we're jotting down notes on the changing seasons or sketching a new bloom in the garden, journaling becomes a meditation—a practice of presence that allows us to cultivate deeper peace and connection.

One of the most useful things I did when I started the farm was keep a journal and record dates of observations and events in the field. Seeing trends helped me home in on what was happening with the soil and the ecosystem each season and to make changes accordingly, yet it also helped me appreciate the subtle nuances of the natural world—the way the sunlight filters through the leaves, the sound of birdsong in early spring. Each entry became a treasure trove of memories, insights, and inspiration—a record of my journey as a steward of the land.

Writing daily (or even weekly) isn't necessary, but it can be beneficial to check back year over year to see general trends in your garden. I like to keep a small notebook and a basic set of watercolor paints in my garden trug for such observations. I always think I will remember the details next year, but memory seems to fail me! These are some of the things I like to keep track of.

Frost and soil temperature patterns. It's fascinating to note weather patterns, especially in spring. I observe that some areas of my garden are colder than others in spring, depending on proximity to structures or elevation, and noting this as it occurs keeps me from losing tender seedlings because I learn to plant cold-tolerant things in those locations. Tracking soil temperatures year over year has taught me when to start seeds for my area. While USDA Hardiness Zone average frost dates give broad sweeps of this information, studying the microclimates within our own gardens greatly boosts our success with planting times.

Pest and beneficials appearances and disappearances. Tracking the appearance of aphids was extremely revealing. I noticed that aphids showed up in spring in areas where nitrogen fertilizer had been applied; clearly, the insects were drawn to the fresh and rapid green growth. This was one of the incentives that spurred me to stop fertilizing and instead start relying on the warming soil microbes to convert organic matter into plant nutrients. Making this change eliminated the rapid growth swings that fertilizing brought and led to decreased numbers of pests. Alongside tracking pests and their timing, I tracked when the beneficial insects arrived—and it was almost like clockwork: Once I spotted aphids in the garden, I noticed that lacewing eggs would appear within about two weeks. Similarly, the timing of baby birds hatching and robins seeking food in the garden coincided with the appearance of caterpillars. Watching and tracking these cycles brought nature's ways into clearer focus and helped me understand that each piece of the garden ecosystem has its own place. With this understanding came a sense of peace: Although the aphids could be frustrating, I knew that applying any sort of pesticide to them would impact the beneficials that would otherwise appear soon. Instead of worrying about "pests," I was able to embrace their presence and understand their larger role as a food source for the adorable ladybugs my children love to find inside the flowers.

Planting dates and seed-starting dates. Using a calendar, I track when I start my seeds and when the seedlings are planted. These dates, along with my soil temperature and frost date information, help me zero in on the best timing for my garden's microclimate. It's a huge timesaver! Each year, instead of trying to remember when I need to start my seeds, I simply reference my planting calendar from the previous year. Tracking my starting dates has taught me, for

A garden journal can be as simple or as aesthetic as you desire. If you enjoy expressing yourself artistically, try adding pressed flowers or watercolors of plants from your garden.

example, that later-sown zinnias struggle less with powdery mildew, and that tomato seedlings planted after the soil has warmed more don't get blight or blossom-end rot like those planted earlier. Noting whether plants struggled in a previous year as a result of being kept in their soil blocks too long before planting, or if temperatures were warm enough that plants could have gone out earlier, helps significantly with seed-starting timing success.

Fertilizers/amendments used. Whenever I apply alfalfa fertilizer, compost tea, compost, or any other amendments to the garden, I track this in my journal so I remember which beds have been amended and with what. Having a large garden, I don't treat every planting bed the same way, so keeping a record of what has been applied allows me to use fewer amendments.

Plants/cover crops. Sketching a simple map of the current year's garden plantings and any cover crops, along with dates planted and terminated, helps maintain biodiversity and good

My daughter and I enjoy observing the garden together.

Reflecting on the work it has taken to get these beautiful blooms and being thankful helps me appreciate the difficulties faced in getting to that point.

crop rotation. By rotating plants and ensuring a wide range of varieties, we minimize pest and disease pressure.

Successes/failures. Keeping tabs on which plants are successful in my garden each year minimizes frustration because I learn which plants just don't do well in my growing conditions or in specific soils. Tracking the success of our lavender, which we planted in two different locations, was particularly helpful. One crop was planted at level ground at the front of the field where the soil was heavier. The second location was at the back, where our soil is sandier and was bermed to assist with drainage. Lavender is known to prefer the latter conditions, but surprisingly, all the lavender plants in the front clay soil survived, while those in the back died off over a particularly cold winter. The varieties we chose combined with cold temperatures meant that the lavender survived better in the clay soil, which held moisture better and protected the roots during the temperature swings of our high altitude. Tracking which varieties perform best also helps us save money and learn which plants thrive in our climate and which aren't worth the difficulty.

Bloom times/gaps in the garden. To support pollination and attract beneficial insects, it is best to have a variety of bloom shapes at all times in the garden: spikes, trumpets, and umbel flowers. Tracking when there are gaps in blooms allows us to adjust and add plants to fill those voids for the subsequent year and maintain consistent levels of beneficial insects throughout the season.

Soil reports and trends. If you have done soil testing, journaling this can be as simple as printing out your soil reports for easy reference. It is easy to get sucked into thinking we need to apply fertilizers when a soil test clearly indicates that we don't! I find that the visual evidence that my soil has sufficient levels of most nutrients keeps me from adding fertilizers when they aren't necessary. Keeping the reports in your journal also makes it easy to see what's happening in the garden over time.

Pressing flowers to keep in a garden journal creates a beautiful reminder of the growing season.

Connection with nature. Journaling in the garden is more than just a means of documentation: It is a pathway to understanding the natural world and our place in it. After all, gardening is as regenerative for our spirit as it is for the soil. As we pour our thoughts and observations onto the page, we create space for growth. Observing closely and considering the deeper relationships between our garden and its surroundings can prompt us to see our homes—and the entire planet—more clearly, and to understand the impact we each have. In the embrace of nature, we find refuge—a sanctuary where we can lay down our burdens and reconnect with our true selves.

As I'm gardening, hearing the birds chirp and breathing in the fresh smell of moist soil, my mind becomes clearer to the light of life. Things come to me that I may forget later if I don't jot them down, or maybe I want to take a moment to do an amateurish sketch or watercolor of a beautiful tomato or flower. I'm sure there are many apps now that allow for tracking what's happening in the garden on smartphones, but there is something so calming about sitting down with your garden journal in winter, paging through it, and planning the coming spring.

Take Time to Connect with Your Garden

Perhaps journaling in the garden is not for you—don't force it! The garden is meant to be regenerative to our spirit and soul, not drudgery. Simply take a moment to breathe deeply, to open your senses to the wonders that surround you. As you wander through your garden, feel the soil beneath your feet, the sun on your skin. No matter how big or small, your garden is your partner on this journey of growth and discovery.

Remember that ecosystem changes and synchronicity will not happen overnight but over a period of several seasons. When you inevitably find yourself feeling frustrated and wanting to reach for a store-bought solution, try taking the 10-mile view of the garden. Step back from the damaged and affected plants. Take five steps back. Then take 10 steps back. Does it really matter that some of the leaves are eaten, some of the fruits affected, some petals missing? From farther away, is the damage worse than the

potential side effect of wiping out our struggling insects? Or could the problem potentially be solved by finding a missing piece of the ecosystem? Remove the burden and expectation of perfection in the garden and embrace the flawed beauty of nature. In the regenerative garden, we find not only peace but purpose—a sense of belonging to something greater than ourselves.

So go forth, dear gardeners. Protect your peace and your planet—cultivate a space that sustains both you and your ecosystem, that heals the soil and also the soul. May your garden be a refuge—a sanctuary of beauty, abundance, and peace. And may we walk this path of regenerative gardening with open hearts and open minds, knowing that by supporting nature, we find both sustenance and solace.

Living the Principles: The Seasonal Guide

Now that we've laid all the foundational understanding and principles of the regenerative ecological garden, we can tackle some specific how-tos! This guide is loosely based on the four seasons to give you an idea of what practices can be implemented and when, to support garden productivity and ecosystem and soil health.

Spring

Waking the Garden

Spring is a thrilling time in any garden, full of vibrancy, the excitement of the season to come, the smell of damp soil, and birds chirping. It's also a very busy time! Here are some to-do items to keep you organized.

Starting new garden beds. Garden beds can be started in early spring and, if set up early enough, can even be planted with a cool-temperature germinating cover crop.

Managing fall-planted cover crops. As soil temperatures begin to warm, check for regrowth of any fall-planted cover crops. If you didn't anticipate regrowth, make a new plan for termination.

Soil testing. If you are planning to test your soil, submit soil tests around a month before planting time. (Alternatively, you can test in fall.) This will give you time to analyze your results and make a plan for the coming season. Whether you submit tests in fall or in spring is up to you, but be sure to do it at the same time each year for the most accurate representation of changes over time.

Planting spring cover crops. In areas that didn't receive a fall cover crop, sow early-spring cover crops such as peas, which can germinate in cold soils, about six to eight weeks before your last frost. Make a plan for termination like cutting, rolling/crimping, or tarping.

Broadforking. Once the soil has warmed and dried, broadfork beds prior to planting to help loosen soil for new roots. Broadfork just to crack the soil; do not turn soil completely over.

Mulching. If you wish to plant early in a bed that was thickly mulched for winter, remove some mulch now to help the soil dry out and warm more quickly.

After planting, wait to mulch until plants have three or more sets of leaves to avoid suffocating small plants. Move aside preexisting mulch, like cover crop residue, to allow a planting space.

Clear mulch away from the base of trees to avoid creating mulch volcanos that can rot the bark of the tree and kill it over time.

Apply heavy mulch in any areas that need smothering to establish a new garden space in fall or in the following year.

Cleaning up the garden. Avoid cleaning up old debris, remaining leaves, or dead stalks and stems from the spring garden for as long as possible. Wait until temperatures have warmed to reach around 55°F (13°C) consistently. Waiting will give nesting pollinators, such as carpenter bees and other insects, a chance to emerge. When we clean up the garden too soon, we may unintentionally discard vital and endangered pieces of our ecosystem that need shelter. Leaving these layers of natural mulch will also help protect the soil microbes from UV rays. So only clean up and remove mulch when necessary, and try to store it in a different area of the garden rather than discarding it entirely.

Deciding which homemade amendments to use. Remember, amendments aren't strictly necessary but can be helpful while establishing a routine of cover cropping and regenerative practices in the garden.

Spring is a great time to make the weed tea recipe (see page 185). Then it will be ready around the time your plants may be ready for a mineral boost or show signs that they need it.

The alfalfa fertilizer recipe (see page 190) can be made quickly and easily and applied just before spring planting while the soil is easily accessible. Remember that some soil tests will indicate whether your soil requires additional nutrients, but other tests will not—when in doubt, err on the side of fewer amendments.

Seed starting. Some seeds are started in late winter, but we start the majority of ours in early spring.

Soil blocking. Sift a batch of soil blocking seed-starting soil (see page 85) so it's ready to go when you start your seeds. Remember, the same recipe can be used for trays or soil blocks. Start seeds according to the schedule you established over winter (see the box below for more).

Direct sowing. Once we hit our average last frost date, we begin direct sowing any seeds that prefer that method, such as squashes, beans, zinnias, and others. If you are in an area that has a lot of bunny, bird, or squirrel pressure that keeps your direct-seeding efforts from being successful, it may be worthwhile to keep a few pieces of burlap or frost fabric around to protect your seeds until they have germinated; you can even leave lightweight frost fabric on the plants until they're a few inches tall.

Providing food sources for birds. As birds return from their southern migrations and begin rearing their young, remember that they need the caterpillars and other garden pests you may see popping up, so resist the urge to kill or remove those insects. Instead, attract birds by keeping a consistent water source and some birdseed in the garden, in a high spot safe from neighborhood predators like outdoor cats.

Spring is a busy time for gardeners and pollinators alike.

Timing Seed Starting

Seed-starting timing can be intimidating, especially if you're anything like me and accumulate dozens of seed packets over the dreary winter. A calendar can be helpful: Start by noting your average last frost date (for us, that is around May 15). From there, work back 4 weeks, 6 weeks, 10 weeks, and 12 weeks, jotting down which seeds need to be started on those dates according to their packet instructions. For example, we typically start our peppers 10 weeks before last frost, so that date on the calendar will list whatever pepper varieties we are starting. This way, we can quickly reference our calendar and know which seeds need starting rather than having to rifle through seed packets continuously!

Summer

Harvesting and Maintaining the Garden

Summer is the time for harvest, preparation for the busy fall, and observation. It is also a time of enjoyment: Don't get so caught up in the rush and intensity of summer in the garden that you get burned out. Dedicate morning coffee time to sitting and calmly observing the garden, journaling, sketching, and enjoying the fruits of your labor. And, of course, eating tomatoes.

Managing weeds through mulching. Weeds thrive over the summer season as soil temperatures warm. Early summer is often dedicated to keeping up with weeds, preventing them from going to seed and spreading, and applying mulches to bare areas to guard against future weed spread and germination.

Planning and planting cover crops. If areas of the garden are bare, or there are areas of poor soil that need extensive regeneration, consider dedicating a growing season to a rotation of cover crops to help build biodiversity and soil organic matter.

Order any cover crops to be planted in late summer or early fall so that as soon as the weather is ideal, you are ready to go—time can be of the essence for establishing that late-summer cover crop, so be prepared!

Composting. The warm temperatures make summer a prime time for composting. If you want finished compost for fall, keep up with a hot compost pile, turning it and keeping it moist to hasten decomposition and have it ready in time.

Providing water for birds and pollinators. A regular water source will help keep birds in the garden. It is important to keep the water clean and constantly filled to encourage birds to remain. Consider having a shallow dish of water with pebbles in it to provide bees with a place to drink without the risk of them drowning; placing it in the garden among the leaves will help your pollinators keep your garden producing without the need to artificially pollinate by hand, which can be time-consuming!

Managing and documenting pests. Summer is when we are most likely to see those so-called pests and their damage in the garden. Record the appearance of pests in your journal and research which beneficials would be good to attract to your garden to help combat them. Incorporate the corresponding beneficial insect–attracting plants into your plans for next season's garden.

Applying amendments. Apply compost tea (see page 186) to help combat disease, fungus, and even pests by supporting the health of the soil and building more vigorous plants. Again, these recipes can be helpful especially in the first years of establishing the regenerative garden and will become mostly unnecessary over years of building the soil food web and ecosystem.

Summer is the time for harvesting and savoring the fruits of your labor.

Fall

Preparing the Garden for Rest

Fall can be a time of exhaustion for the gardener. After a busy season, we are usually ready for the oncoming frost and even welcome it, but try to keep your energy up and end strong! That said, remember that you can start a cover crop and cut down plants if you are feeling ready to be done with your garden. This can help prevent creeping garden burnout, so give yourself that option if you feel impending fatigue.

Planting fall cover crops. In late summer and early fall, planting a cover crop will supply the garden with organic matter, provide living plant roots for your soil food web, prevent erosion, and create a living soil cover.

Using compost (or not). If your compost is ready by fall, this can be a good time to apply it to beds so that it breaks down and is worked into the soil by microbes. Similarly, if you incorporate animals into your regenerative garden, applying their partially composted bedding/manure now allows time for any salinity to leach out through winter snows and rains and for the organic matter to age and break down by spring.

Remember that if your soil test reported high levels of phosphorus, however, you will want to use caution with compost, particularly animal-based compost.

Making and collecting your soil "blankets." Soil does not like to be left bare over the winter season. Not only does exposure subject soil microbes to fluctuations in temperature and moisture level, it increases the risk of erosion and of early-spring weeds taking hold. Autumn is the time to blanket the soil with straw, leaves (weighed down with a frost fabric or tarp), grass clippings, or other mulch of your choice to help protect the soil life.

New plantings of natives, perennials, and trees. Early fall can be an excellent time to plant new perennials and trees, allowing them to establish their root system during the often more temperate fall weather, before winter freezes set in. In more temperate climates, fall plantings allow for earlier spring harvests with overwintering cold-tolerant plants such as kale, spinach, carrots, and others.

Creating habitat for ecosystem support over winter. Make a few small piles of sticks, brush, leaves, or garden debris to provide winter shelter for bird populations and insects.

Seed saving. At the farm, we harvest many of our seeds in late fall and early winter, depending on the plant. Some plants' seeds are ready for harvest earlier than this. While we leave most of our seed heads for winter bird forage, we are careful to save enough seed to expand our garden and replace any plants that die off. We do this once the seeds are dried and easily fall from the plant, indicating that they have fully ripened. Store seeds in a cool place until you are ready to start seedlings.

Crafting a plan for wind and erosion protection. My region gets strong fall and winter winds that can erode mulches, so I like having a backup of frost fabric or a tarp to help weigh down winter covers in the event of extreme winds.

Cover sensitive plants like climbing roses with burlap. Wrap tree trunks of newer trees to prevent temperature fluctuations that can split bark and kill young trees.

After the last frost's winterkill, we prefer to leave as much debris in place as possible. Old stems and seeds provide bird forage in winter and a nesting place for native solitary pollinators such as mason bees.

Remove any vegetation that was diseased, then discard it in the trash (do not compost) to avoid spreading the disease to plants in the next season.

Winter

Reflection, Rest, and Planning

Winter can be a time of rest and quiet. After all those fall preparations, it's okay to take a break from the garden; don't think on it for a while, if that's what you need. When you feel ready and gardening sounds enticing again, begin your spring planning. While winter can offer a break from the garden, it can also be a wonderfully quiet time to focus on preparation.

Winter watering. For any newer plantings or young trees, consider winter watering one or two times per month if temperatures are above 40°F (4°C) and the soil is thawed. Keeping the soil around roots moist will help prevent damage from extreme cold temperatures and freezes.

Planning for next year's garden. Planning is one of the most enjoyable parts of gardening! Sit down and review your garden journal from the past season and pinpoint what changes could be made to better support the garden ecosystem. Which insects were particularly troublesome? What rotations of plants will discourage ongoing pests such as squash vine borers? (Perhaps it is time to take a break for a season on squash if the pests have been particularly bad, for example.)

Making a garden map. If you are just beginning your garden, make your garden map and include existing plants/trees, soil information, and structures in your layout (see page 139). Don't forget to include pathways!

Plan and organize seed-starting timing. Create your seed-starting calendar and organize your seeds. I like to divide seed packets into groups organized by start-by dates (12, 10, 8, 6, and 4 weeks before last frost), as well as seeds that need direct sowing and when. Then I put them all in an old shoebox, mason jars, or a photo organizer box from a craft store. This allows me to quickly and easily grab the seeds that need starting on a given date.

Purchasing seeds. Whenever possible, purchase seeds from a seed company near your ecoregion that is growing and saving as many of their own seeds as possible. Ask where seeds are sourced. Seeds that are grown and harvested in regions similar to yours will have the best success.

Creating goals for your garden. Is this the year you plan on creating a cutting garden for yourself? Are you focusing on foods your family actually wants to eat? Foods that can be stored and canned? What did you not enjoy growing last season? Being realistic with what aspects and plants you enjoy will help you be more mindful with what you grow.

Accumulating seed-starting and soil blocking supplies. You don't want to be scrambling in spring to pull together your supplies, so order them in winter and set them aside. If you are going to try soil blocking, perhaps practice a bit so you feel confident with the method.

Remember, do not overdo it in winter. Many of us are busy with holidays and are just burned out from the past gardening season. Let yourself embrace a time of quiet and absence from the garden for as long as needed, then dive in when you feel rejuvenated and energized to tackle planning!

Think ahead to spring as the garden rests in winter.

Guide to the Latin Names of Plants

agastache (*Agastache rupestris*)
alfalfa (*Medicago sativa*)
American bittersweet (*Celastrus scandens*)
American plum (*Prunus americana)*
American wisteria (*Wisteria frutescens*)
anise hyssop (*Agastache foeniculum*)
annual buckwheat (*Eriogonum annuum*)
annual ryegrass (*Lolium multiflorum*)
aster (*Symphyotrichum* spp.)

bachelor's button (*Centaurea cyanus*)
baptisia (*Baptisia* spp.)
bee balm (*Monarda* spp.)
Bermuda grass (*Cynodon dactylon*)
black chokeberry (*Aronia melanocarpa*)
blueberry (*Vaccinium* spp.)
blue flax (*Linum lewisii*)
blue grama (*Bouteloua gracilis*)
bunchberry (*Cornus* spp.)
burdock (*Arctium minus*)
burning bush (*Euonymus alatus*)
bush honeysuckle (*Lonicera* spp.)
butterfly bush, buddleia (*Buddleja davidii*)

Canada thistle (*Cirsium arvense*)
Chinese wisteria (*Wisteria sinensis*)
chokecherry (*Prunus virginiana*)
cilantro (*Coriandrum sativum*)
climbing hydrangea (*Decumaria barbara*)
common bean (*Phaseolus vulgaris*)
common boneset (*Eupatorium perfoliatum*)
common buckthorn (*Rhamnus cathartica*)
common buckwheat (*Fagopyrum esculentum*)
common mallow (*Malva neglecta*)
common sunflower (*Helianthus annuus*)
common wheat (*Triticum aestivum*)
common yarrow (*Achillea millefolium*)
coreopsis, tickseed (*Coreopsis* spp.)
corn (*Zea mays*)
cowpea (*Vigna unguiculata*)
coyote brush (*Baccharis pilularis*)
creeping bellflower (*Campanula rapunculoides*)
creeping phlox (*Phlox subulata*)
creeping veronica (*Veronica filiformis* and/or *Veronica hederifolia*)
crimson clover (*Trifolium incarnatum*)
cucumber (*Cucumis sativus*)
Culver's root (*Veronicastrum virginicum*)
cup plant, compass plant (*Silphium perfoliatum*)
currants (*Ribes*)

dame's rocket, sweet rocket (*Hesperis matronalis*)
dandelion (*Taraxacum officinale*)
dahlia (*Dahlia* spp.)
dill (*Anethum graveolens*)

echinacea, coneflower (*Echinacea* spp.)
English ivy (*Hedera helix*)

false aster (*Boltonia asteroides*)
fava bean (*Vicia faba*)
fennel (*Foeniculum vulgare*)
field bindweed (*Convolvulus arvensis*)
field pea, winter pea (*Pisum sativum* subsp. *arvense*)
field pussytoes (*Antennaria neglecta*)
forsythia (*Forsythia* spp.)

geranium (*Geranium* spp.)
golden alexanders (*Zizia aurea*)
golden currant (*Ribes aureum*)
goldenrod (*Solidago* spp.)

hairy vetch (*Vicia villosa*)
heart-leaved meadow parsnip, heartleaf alexanders (*Zizia aptera*)
hoary cress (*Lepidium draba*)
hoary vervain (*Verbena stricta*)
hydrangea (*Hydrangea* spp.)

Japanese barberry (*Berberis thunbergii*)
Japanese honeysuckle (*Lonicera japonica*)
Japanese knotweed (*Fallopia japonica, Polygonum cuspidatum*)
Joe-Pye weed (*Eutrochium* spp.)
johnsongrass (*Sorghum halepense*)

kale (*Brassica oleracea* var. *acephala*)
kudzu (*Pueraria montana* var. *lobata*)

lacy phacelia, fiddleneck (*Phacelia tanacetifolia*)
lavender (*Lavandula* spp.)
leafy spurge (*Euphorbia esula*)

lentil (*Lens culinaris*)
lettuce (*Lactuca sativa*)
lisianthus (*Eustoma grandiflorum*)
little bluestem (*Schizachyrium scoparium*)
low calamint (*Clinopodium arkansanum*)

marigold (*Tagetes* spp.)
microclover (*Trifolium repens*)
milkweed (*Asclepias* spp.)
moss phlox (*Phlox subulata*)
mountain mint (*Pycnanthemum* spp.)
mountain spurge (*Pachysandra procumbens*)
multiflora rose (*Rosa multiflora*)
mustard (*Brassica* spp.)

nasturtium (*Tropaeolum majus*)
New Jersey tea (*Ceanothus americanus*)
ninebark (*Physocarpus* spp.)
nodding onion (*Allium cernuum*)

oat, spring oat (*Avena sativa*)
onion (*Allium cepa*)
oriental bittersweet (*Celastrus orbiculatus*)

Palmer's penstemon (*Penstemon palmeri*)
pearly everlasting (*Anaphalis margaritacea*)
peony (*Paeonia* spp.)
pepper (*Capsicum annuum*)
perennial phlox (*Phlox paniculata*)
periwinkle (*Vinca minor*)
petunia (*Petunia* spp.)
pigweed amaranth (*Amaranthus retroflexus*)
pinnate prairie coneflower, gray-headed coneflower (*Ratibida pinnata*)
plantain (*Plantago* spp.)
porcelain berry (*Ampelopsis brevipedunculata*)
pumpkin (*Cucurbita pepo*)
purple loosestrife (*Lythrum salicaria*)

Queen Anne's lace, chocolate lace flower (*Daucus carota*)

radish, oilseed radish, daikon (*Raphanus sativus*)
rapeseed (*Brassica napus*)
Rocky Mountain penstemon (*Penstemon strictus*)
rose (*Rosa* spp.)
rosemary (*Salvia rosmarinus, Rosmarinus officinalis*)
rudbeckia (*Rudbeckia* spp.)

sedum (*Sedum* spp.)
seven-son flower (*Heptacodium miconioides*)
shrubby cinquefoil (*Dasiphora fruticosa* subsp. *Floribunda*)
Siberian elm (*Ulmus pumila*)
smooth brome (*Bromus inermis*)
smooth oxeye (*Heliopsis helianthoides*)
snapdragon (*Antirrhinum majus*)
snap pea (*Pisum sativum*)
snow-in-summer (*Cerastium tomentosum*)
sorghum-Sudan grass (*Sorghum bicolor* × *S. bicolor* var. *sudanese*)
spotted bee balm, horsemint (*Monarda punctata*)
squash (*Cucurbita* spp.)
strawberry (*Fragaria* × *ananassa*)
Sudan grass (*Sorghum* × *drummondii*)
Sunn hemp (*Crotalaria juncea*)
swamp milkweed (*Asclepias incarnata*)
sweet alyssum (*Lobularia maritima*)
sweet autumn clematis (*Clematis terniflora*)
sweet pea (*Lathyrus odoratus*)
sweet potato (*Ipomoea batatas*)
switchgrass (*Panicum virgatum*)

thistle (*Cirsium* spp.)
timothy (*Phleum pratense*)
tomato (*Solanum lycopersicum*)
tree of heaven (*Ailanthus altissima*)
turnip, forage turnip (*Brassica rapa*)

viburnum (*Viburnum* spp.)
Virginia sweetspire (*Itea virginica*)
virgin's bower (*Clematis virginiana*)

white meadowsweet (*Spiraea alba*)
white top (*Lepidium draba*)
wild ginger (*Asarum canadense*)
winter rye (*Secale cereale*)
woodland strawberry (*Fragaria vesca*)

yarrow (*Achillea millefolium*)
yerba mansa (*Anemopsis californica*)

zinnia (*Zinnia* spp.)

Further Reading

Brown, Gabe. *Dirt to Soil: One Family's Journey into Regenerative Agriculture*. Chelsea Green Publishing, 2018.

Lowenfels, Jeff. *Teaming with Bacteria: The Organic Gardener's Guide to Endophytic Bacteria and the Rhizophagy Cycle*. Timber Press, 2022.

———. *Teaming with Fungi: The Organic Grower's Guide to Mycorrhizae*. Timber Press, 2017.

Lowenfels, Jeff, and Wayne Lewis. *Teaming with Microbes: The Organic Gardener's Guide to the Soil Food Web*. Timber Press, 2010.

Montgomery, David R. *Growing a Revolution: Bringing Our Soil Back to Life*. W. W. Norton & Company, 2017.

Savory, Allan, and Jody Butterfield. *Holistic Management: A Commonsense Revolution to Restore Our Environment*. Island Press, 2016.

Tallamy, Douglas W. *Bringing Nature Home: How Native Plants Sustain Wildlife in Our Gardens*. Timber Press, 2007.

———. *Nature's Best Hope: A New Approach to Conservation That Starts in Your Yard*. Timber Press, 2020.

Vogt, Benjamin. *A New Garden Ethic: Cultivating Defiant Compassion for an Uncertain Future*. New Society Publishers, 2017.

Retailers and Nurseries

BROADFORKS

Mindful Farmer
https://mindfulfarmerarkansas.com

Treadlite Broadforks
https://treadlitebroadforks.com

MYCORRHIZAE AND INOCULANTS

Advancing Eco Agriculture
https://advancingecoag.com

Big Foot Microbes
https://bigfootmyco.com

Dr. Earth
https://drearth.com

NATIVE PLANT INFO

Native Plant Finder
https://nativeplantfinder.nwf.org

PEAT-FREE SOIL

FoxFarm "Coco Loco"
https://foxfarm.com

SOIL BLOCKERS

Ladbrooke
https://soilblockers.co.uk

Swiftblocker
https://swiftblocker.com

SOIL TESTING

Regen Ag Lab
https://regenaglab.com

Ward Laboratories, Inc.
https://wardlab.com

WOOL PELLETS

Sustaina Grow
https://sustainagrow.co.nz

Wild Valley Farms
https://wildvalleyfarms.com

Metric Conversion Charts

WEIGHT

To convert	to	multiply
pounds	grams	pounds by 453.5
pounds	kilograms	pounds by 0.45

VOLUME

To convert	to	multiply
teaspoons	milliliters	teaspoons by 4.93
tablespoons	milliliters	tablespoons by 14.79
cups	milliliters	cups by 236.59
cups	liters	cups by 0.24
quarts	liters	quarts by 0.946
gallons	liters	gallons by 3.785

US	Metric
1 teaspoon	5 milliliters
1 tablespoon	15 milliliters
1 cup	240 milliliters
4 cups (1 quart)	0.95 liter
4 quarts (1 gallon)	3.8 liters

TEMPERATURE

To convert	to	
Fahrenheit	Celsius	subtract 32 from Fahrenheit temperature, multiply by 5, then divide by 9

AREA

1 acre = 4046.86 square meters

1 acre = 0.404686 hectares

LENGTH

To convert	to	multiply
inches	millimeters	inches by 25.4
inches	centimeters	inches by 2.54
feet	meters	feet by 0.3048
feet	kilometers	feet by 0.0003048
yards	centimeters	yards by 91.44
yards	meters	yards by 0.9144
yards	kilometers	yards by 0.0009144
miles	kilometers	miles by 1.609344

US (inches)	Metric (centimeters)
0.5	1.27
1	2.54
1.5	3.81
2	5.08
2.5	6.35
3	7.62
3.5	8.89
4	10.16
4.5	11.43
5	12.70
5.5	13.97
6	15.24
6.5	16.51
7	17.78
7.5	19.05
8	20.32
8.5	21.59
9	22.86
9.5	24.13
10	25.40

Index

Page numbers in *italics* indicate photographs and numbers in **bold** indicate charts.

S

T